103 Questions

Youth Workers Ask

John O. Gooch

DISCIPLESHIP RESOURCES

PO BOX 340003 • NASHVILLE, TN 37203-0003
www.discipleshipresources.org

*For Beth, who was at home while I
was doing all these workshops and
supported me enthusiastically in the
writing of this book. Thanks.*

Cover and book design by Joey McNair

Edited by Debra D. Smith and Heidi L. Hewitt

ISBN 0-88177-405-7

Library of Congress Control Number 2003101982

The quotation from the Baptismal Covenant I on page 85 is from *The United Methodist Hymnal*, page 34. Copyright © 1976, 1980, 1985, 1989 The United Methodist Publishing House. Used by permission.

Scripture quotations, unless otherwise indicated, are from the New Revised Standard Version of the Bible, copyright © 1989 by the Division of Christian Education of the National Council of the Churches of Christ in the USA. All rights reserved. Used by permission.

DR405

Contents

Introduction

Why 103 questions? Hey, because anyone can do 100 questions. We wanted something more.

That something more is based on questions that have actually been asked by youth workers in workshops and seminars that I have led around the country. At the beginning of workshops, I distributed three-by-five index cards and asked the participants to write down the questions and concerns they had. The rule was one question to a card. (Index cards are cheap, and that way I could sort them out easily.) After several years of doing workshops, I had a large stack of index cards, each with its question. That stack of cards was the starting point for this book. Some questions in the book were not asked in those workshops. Some of them came from staff members at the General Board of Discipleship. Others, which are listed as "Questions You Didn't Ask," are foundational issues that should be addressed by all of us at some point in our ministries with youth. But the heart of the book is the list of questions that youth workers asked.

The questions were cries for help. People genuinely wanted to know how to and why to do many different things in youth ministry. This may have been the most important impression I carried away from all those workshops. People genuinely care about youth and want to do the best

11

possible job of ministering to and with youth. But people are also scared: What if I fail? What if I don't do a good job? What will happen?

Youth ministry focuses critical questions for us in several different ways. First, we know there is a lot at stake in what we do. We are concerned about what is happening to youth in today's world. We know about drugs, alcohol, sexual activity, and other kinds of high-risk behaviors that tempt youth. We know how crucial it is that youth have a solid background so that they can stand firm against temptation and can mature into dependable, solid adults. We also know that the Christian faith is only a generation away from extinction, and a key part of preserving the faith is in the hands of those of us who do youth ministry. We desperately want to pass onto youth the teachings of the faith and an understanding of the importance of being Christian in today's world. Since there is a lot at stake, we sometimes care so much that we get in our own way.

Second, youth ministry is incarnational. Who we are and how we act may be even more important than what we teach. We do not want to turn youth off from the faith because who we are screams so loudly they cannot hear what we say. So, we want to be sure we do things right. Beyond the immediate fears of messing up, there is also a strong theological component to incarnational ministry. After all, the heart of Christian faith is that, as St. Irenaeus said, "[God] became what we are so that we could become what [God] is" (my translation; from "Irenaeus Against Heresies," Book V, in *The Ante-Nicene Fathers: The Writings of the Fathers Down to* A.D. *325, Volume I,* page 526; William B. Eerdmans Publishing Co., reprint 1973). Two thousand years after the birth of Jesus of Nazareth, we cannot see God with our own eyes. But we know that one of the places where youth see God is in the lives of adults around them. The more important the adult is in their lives, the more important it is that they see God in that adult. For many youth, the important adults in their lives are those of us who work with them in youth ministry. No wonder we are scared of making a big mistake. A lot is at stake.

Third, most of us feel that we are ill-equipped and inadequate for the ministry that we try to carry out. Take me as an example. I began doing youth ministry in the local church more than forty years ago. I have been a leader in youth ministry on the district, conference, and jurisdictional levels and have directed church camps for years. Then I went to Nashville and served on the youth ministry staff of the General Board of Discipleship, where I developed youth curriculum resources, helped plan national events, and led training workshops all over the country. Most recently, in semi-retirement, I am again working in youth ministry, as a volunteer in the local church. I ought to be equipped for ministry, right? And yet, each Sunday I am aware of how much more I need to know in order to be effective with youth. Each of us continues to learn and grow in who we are and what we do.

So, for all of us, this book is about how to do youth ministry. You will not find much here in the way of theology or Bible, although I believe that theology and biblical knowledge is critical for youth ministry. That is the topic of another book. This book is basic how-tos, with some why-tos thrown in.

This book is the result of more than forty years of doing youth ministry and more than fifteen years training youth ministers. Most of what I know about youth ministry I have learned from them. My thanks go to all those youth ministers with whom I have talked over the years and miles. I am grateful for the questions they have raised that ultimately became this book. My friends in youth ministry have pushed me to think more about our common ministry and to search for answers to the most important questions with which we deal. Thanks to Tammy Shelton for help with Safe Sanctuaries materials. My special thanks go to colleagues and friends like Walt Marcum, Kenda Creasy Dean, Brian Hardesty-Crouch, Sandy Miller, Robin Pippin, Charles Harrison, Chris Hughes, Susan King, Ron and Celia Whitler, Mike Ratliff, Mike Selleck, Lynn Hutton, Tom Salsgiver, Chuck Kishpaugh, Joy Allen, and Rod Hocott. The long hours we have talked together have helped me work through both ideas and practical solutions. They have given me opportunities to do workshops, to be in conversation with other youth workers, and to teach both the theology and the practice of youth ministry. Their wisdom and experience have greatly enriched my understanding and, in turn, the content of this book. Any errors, of course, remain my own. Finally, I want to express my deep appreciation to the Family and Life Span Team at the General Board of Discipleship of The United Methodist Church for their interest in making this book a reality. MaryJane Pierce Norton initiated the conversation, and Susan Hay gave enthusiastic support. Debra Smith is an excellent editor, and I appreciate her skill in shaping the final form.

John Gooch
Liberty, Missouri
December 2002

Building Christian Community

Building Christian community is one of the most critical tasks we face in youth ministry. Through Christian community we transmit the faith and form disciples, strengthening them to go out in mission and ministry. We want youth in the group to relate to one another so that we can do programming, mission, service, and so forth. Community is important for what it models biblically and theologically. The faith story of the Bible is built on community. It begins with the people of Israel coming out of Egyptian slavery and slowly beginning to form a community under the leadership of Moses, Miriam, and Aaron. The rest of the Old Testament story is about the people of God struggling to live in community faithfully and creatively. The fact that the struggle often ended in failure and disappointment does not make community any less critical or urgent. In the New Testament, Paul reminds us that the Christian community is nothing less than the body of Christ, a powerful image for community. Paul, Peter, James, and John all write about the importance of the community and offer practical, as well as theological, guidance for living together in a community of faith.

Our youth are a part of that long line of people who worked and prayed within the context of the community we call the church. The key to what we do in building community is inviting youth to become a part of that community of faith.

How do I establish one-on-one relationships with youth?

Youth ministry, perhaps more than any other kind of ministry, is incarnational—that is, it is about God with skin on. You and other adults who work with youth are the skin. So, one-on-one relationships are important, probably more important than interesting programs and exciting trips.

With some youth, relationships just happen. You greet them, and you have instant rapport with them. But this is rare, as most relationships take more time to develop. Here are some things that will help build relationships.

1. Be patient. Just as Rome was not built in a day, neither are relationships. Make an effort to learn each youth's name, grade in school, special interests, and so forth. Talk to youth when you see them in the halls at church, on the street, or at their workplaces.

2. Make time in your Sunday school lesson or fellowship program to ask, "How did it go this week?" Ask what was really good or really bad. Listen carefully to what youth say. If you sense that a youth needs to talk about an issue, arrange a time to get together.

3. Take relationships one at a time. You may be working on many relationships at the same time, but you can grow them only one at a time. When you have an opportunity to develop a personal relationship, focus on that youth for that moment in time. As you develop personal relationships with youth, remember to always follow your congregation's policies for Safe Sanctuaries (see Question 97).

4. Be a participant, not an observer, in community-building activities. You can work on relationships as your team works to solve a problem. That will never happen if you are on the sidelines.

5. Be aware that you may never develop close relationships with some youth. However, another adult worker may be able to. Remember that you are part of a team, so you do not have to do everything.

6. Continue to pray for youth by name, one at a time. The act of prayer makes you more open to them, more comfortable when you are with them, and more willing to risk yourself in a relationship. Prayer also opens doors to relationships with the youth for whom you pray.

16

2 How do we make youth ministry personal in a large church?

The key is to have a large team of adults who all work at developing relationships and making ministry personal. If the adult workers meet together regularly and talk about how they relate with youth, you will begin to discover which youth are outside the relationship sphere. Then one or more adults can make a commitment to developing a relationship with those youth. No youth worker can have a close personal relationship with every youth in a large church. In very large churches, the professional youth workers may not have a great deal of week-to-week contact with all the youth. Personal relationships are developed by volunteers who work with small groups within the large ministry, and the professional youth worker supports and resources the volunteers. Even in this situation, however, the youth minister can know the names of youth, know something about them and their families, and be able to engage in conversation with them on a personal level (beyond saying, "Hi. How's it goin'?").

3 How do we keep youth from falling through the cracks?

Begin with something so obvious that it seems silly: Keep good attendance records. I may think Sally has been at youth group two Sundays this month, but a look at the records will tell me she has missed six weeks in a row. You have to have solid information before you can plan for action.

When any youth has missed twice in a row without a good reason (such as a trip with family), it is time for postcards, e-mails, phone calls, or however you communicate with the youth in your group. This does not have to be a major production, just a quick note or call to let the youth know he or she is missed. If possible, add a note about something special you really miss when that person is not there: "I miss your smile" or "You always help shy youth. They really miss you."

Be persistent. If your first note or call does not bring results, try again. If that does not work, try a personal visit (remembering all the parameters about Safe Sanctuaries; see Question 97). Persistence is crucial. In a slightly different context, when I was a youth I invited one of my friends to come to youth group. The youth did not come. So, knowing something about how one gets results, I told him I would come by the next Sunday night to pick him up. He said he was not ready. I told him to be ready the next week, and I would be by again. It took thirteen weeks before he was ready when I came by. After that, he never missed a youth meeting, Sunday school class, or worship unless he was sick. Today, he is the lay leader of his church.

Make youth ministry personal. Know youth and what is happening with them (see Questions 1 and 2). To keep youth from falling through the cracks, you have to be constantly alert and working to stay in touch.

How do we engage those who do not want to be in the group but have to be there?

These are the youth whose parents say things such as, "You will stay in Sunday school until you finish confirmation" or "You have to go to youth group. It will be good for you, and you'll make lots of friends." That theme has about a dozen more variations, and you may have heard most of them. So, how *do* you engage those youth?

Do not make them self-conscious about their situation by singling them out or by talking about their situation. If they want to talk about it, they will come to you. Most of the time, however, they communicate with an attitude that lets you know what they are thinking: *Okay, I'm here. My parents can make me come, but you can't make me like it.*

If you have a Sunday school class or youth group where youth are actively involved, these "you can't make me" youth may become engaged in spite of themselves. However, they also need some special attention. Ask them what they really like and how they like to learn (see Questions 22 and 94). Do not make a big deal about them having to be there. Focus your conversation on them: what is happening in their lives and what is fun for them. Invite them to help with leadership in an area in which they are interested. Encourage them to be involved in retreats, mission projects, and other activities that are purely voluntary.

Challenge them to engage in things they do not have to do. If their parents force them to come to Sunday school or youth group, challenge them to volunteer to become part of a Bible study group or prayer group that meets during the week. They may become more involved if the activity is something they can freely choose. Sometimes these youth are bored by Sunday school and/or youth group and need a group that challenges

18

their minds. The invitation to become part of a small group that goes deeper may be exactly what they have been waiting for.

5 What about youth with special needs? We have a boy who is deaf and a foreign exchange student who needs our youth to speak more slowly so that she can keep up with the conversation.

Those are two kinds of special needs. Others include dyslexia, attention deficit disorder (ADD), and physical or mental challenges.

An important part of building community is including everyone in as many activities as possible. People with special needs may need some help, but the help should come, as much as possible, from the group without making a big deal of it. For example, if you have a youth in a wheelchair and your activity involves a trust walk, or a low-ropes activity, you may have to modify the activity slightly so that the person in the wheelchair can participate. Other youth can be responsible for helping get the wheelchair around outdoors. The key is that every youth is responsible for the well-being of all the other youth in the group.

If you have a youth with dyslexia or some other learning disorder, do not expect that youth to read the Scripture for your devotional time. Find other ways to be sure that he or she is learning and participating. Maybe more of the learning can be verbal, rather than a lot of reading. With attention deficit disorder, you may need to structure more learning activities that are active, rather than passive (see Questions 22 and 94). One church with a youth who was deaf made arrangements for the signer for worship to come to Sunday school and translate the lesson. The signer also helped the other youth in the class learn some basic signs so that they could say hello and carry on simple conversations in sign language. This not only helped the youth who was hearing impaired to become a part of the group but also helped build community in the rest of the group as well. Obviously, not every group will have access to a skilled signer. Check around in the community for people who can sign.

With foreign exchange students, who need people to speak more slowly, the leader sets the example. When you teach or give directions for an activity, speak slowly and distinctly. If youth talk too fast and low, stop them and say something such as, "I hear as well as I ever did. I just don't hear as fast. Could you repeat that a little more slowly, please?" If you can say that *you* need them to talk more slowly, you will have helped your exchange student without calling attention to her or him.

19

How do we help new youth feel at home?

Whether it is Sunday school or youth group, take time to introduce new youth to the group. Give names and, if possible, something of interest about each youth in the group so that the new person has something to remember. Or have youth introduce themselves by name and tell something that is interesting about themselves. Ask two youth to take the new person under their wings and help him or her begin to feel comfortable. This is particularly important for fellowship groups, where the pattern of the evening may vary from church to church. Knowing such things as how to get ready for snacks or supper, what to expect from fellowship time, and what to bring to the worship circle can help new youth avoid a lot of embarrassment and feel more at home. Youth are the best people to provide that kind of guidance, one step at a time. Asking youth to take responsibility for newcomers also helps build a sense of community among the whole group.

If this is a new idea for you, carefully select youth to mentor newcomers so that the first steps will be successful ones. Other group members will learn by watching what they should do to welcome newcomers. Then other youth can begin to share the responsibility. The added advantage of this approach is that if you choose leaders in the group to welcome newcomers, this carries the subtle, unspoken message that it is okay to be open to new people in the group.

How do we handle cliques?

Cliques can be one of the most destructive elements to community in any group. Surprisingly, cliques can also be an element in building community. It depends on how the clique functions.

So, the first step is to identify which sort of clique you have. A constructive clique is a small group of people who enjoy one another's company, seek one another out, and spend time together without excluding others. Although they do not shut anyone out of their smaller group, they may not go out of their way to make them welcome, either. However, they welcome other people to the youth group. They cheerfully work in small groups with youth not in their clique and do not fuss about being separated.

A destructive clique, on the other hand, is a group of people who want to be together for everything and do not want to be separated for anything. They are exclusive, tend to cut others who venture into their

20

orbit, and complain loudly when you want to break them up, no matter for what reason or for how long. You cannot just ignore them and let their clique continue to eat away at the group like acid.

So, which sort of clique do you have? If it is a constructive clique, do not worry about it. Everyone prefers the company of some people to that of others. As long as they continue to function as a part of the total youth group, welcome others, and do not fuss about being separated for activities, they are not a problem.

If you have a destructive clique, you need to do something. Sometimes it seems as if the only way to open up these groups is by using dynamite. Lectures about the dangers of being a clique and the importance of community do not touch them, since they have a community in which they feel comfortable. What you can do is gently but firmly continue to spread them out among small groups when you do learning or working activities. When they protest that they want to be with their friends, assure them that you recognize that reality and that they will be able to be together later in the meeting (or service project). But right now they are needed in this small group, and you want them to work at finding something good to say about every person in the group.

A wise leader in an adult service organization said that if you act as if you like people in the group, pretty soon you will. The same thing may be true of cliques. If they act as if they are open to dealing with other people, sooner or later they will be. It will be hard and will take a lot of patience and determination on your part, but it will pay off in the end.

How do we mesh kids from different school districts when the only time they see one another is at church? If even a large minority of the group comes from one school, they dominate the group because they know one another.

A good biblical foundation for helping mesh youth from different schools is to focus on the Pauline image of the church as the body of Christ (1 Corinthians 12). Paul was dealing with two issues. The first was that some members of the church were saying that their spiritual gifts were more important than those of others. The second was how to mesh all those different people together into one group. Try some learning activities involving art that tries to show the body as all one organ, such as an eye. Ask pointed questions about how a body could breathe, eat, or do anything else except see if it were an eye. Ask youth what they think Paul

21

was trying to say to the Corinthian church with those images. You probably will not have to point out the obvious parallels to your own group.

One congregation, which had youth from twenty-two different schools in their youth groups, tried making a large wall decoration. At the top of the wall, they put a banner with the words "You are all one in Christ Jesus" and "First Church UMYF." They invited youth to bring school pennants or other emblems that identified their school. The church displayed them on the wall below the banner. (Even if fifteen youth were from one school, only one emblem represented that school.) This decoration was left up all year to remind youth every time they came together that they had both different identities and a common identity.

The key is to focus on the things youth have in common: They face the same problems in growing up. They have similar problems in school; the problems just have different names in different schools. They are all coming to the same youth group. What does that mean for them? If programming for fellowship groups can focus on common needs and interests, meshing becomes much easier.

An excellent resource for building community, and for meshing youth from different schools, is *Go For It!: 25 Faith-Building Adventures for Groups,* by Walt Marcum (Abingdon Press, 1998). It is a collection of twenty-five faith-building adventures that require teamwork and focus on community building through faith. Each adventure has a Bible study as part of the reflection on the activity. It is a good start for meshing youth from different schools into one group.

9. All our youth go to the same school and seem unwilling to be open and vulnerable with one another. What do we do?

Ah, the opposite problem. They have to see one another again on Monday, and they may not all run in the same group at school. They are afraid that something they say will get back to kids at school, who will use it to make fun of them or to gain an advantage. That is a real concern for youth who may be extra sensitive or insecure about their place in the world. What can you do about it?

No youth, in any group, is going to be open and vulnerable without sensing a certain level of trust and community in the group. Community-building activities, such as those in *Go For It!* (see Question 8), can help build the trust level. If openness and vulnerability is an important goal for you, begin moving toward it by discussing topics that are safe. As

22

youth discuss these topics, you can begin asking for personal opinions. This is also the time to begin developing some rules for dialogue. One youth teacher told his class that an important rule was no putdowns, and that he expected the class to make sure that rule was followed by everyone—including him. Several weeks later, he deliberately used a putdown on a person in the class whom he knew could handle it. No one said anything, so he asked them why they did not enforce the rule on him. After that, the youth were clear about the rule against putdowns. In an atmosphere where youth routinely put one another down, the level of openness and vulnerability will always be low.

At a more basic level, it is important that you ask yourselves these questions: Why is openness and vulnerability an important goal for us? What do we mean by openness and vulnerability? How does openness and vulnerability work out at different age levels? Openness is a different thing among sixth graders than among twelfth graders. Being vulnerable is hard for people of all ages, but older youth have, for the most part, more maturity and can handle the risks of vulnerability better than younger youth can.

How do we help those who are excluded by the group?

A question that immediately comes to mind is, Why are they excluded? It may be a question you will have to answer in order to know how to help them. Is it because they are different somehow? Does their behavior invite exclusion? What is the real reason? If there are youth who are not being excluded but who have a good understanding of the group, maybe you could say, "I notice Jamie is always on the outside of the group. What's happening there?"

What form does the exclusion take? Is it simply ignoring the person? Or does it involve verbal putdowns? Do youth physically distance themselves from this person?

Active-learning games help all youth understand what it means to be shut out of the group. Community-building activities (see Question 8) help open some doors. When youth have to depend on a person they have previously excluded, they begin to look at that person in a different way. Biblically and theologically, the imagery of the body of Christ is an important tool for opening the doors to those who are excluded.

While you are patiently working to open doors and have barriers come down, continue to make yourself available to the youth who are being excluded. Make an extra effort to include them in activities. Ask them direct questions in discussion times so that they are invited into the discussion. Encourage them to take leadership roles that can make them look good as they make a contribution to the group.

11 How do we teach youth to have respect for one another and for adults who do not agree with them?

This question sounds as if it is a discipline issue, but it is about building community. Trust and respect are the foundations of any solid group, particularly for a faith community. If snide remarks and comments, such as "That's a stupid question," are the norm for a group, there will be little sense of community—and little hope of ever helping these youth grow in the faith.

You teach respect primarily by example, but sometimes you have to stop and explain it as you go along. As a youth leader and teacher, my primary rule was no putdowns, which was rigidly enforced. Sometimes, the best way to deal with putdowns and other forms of disrespect is to stop the group and say, "Let's see if we can reconstruct what happened in the last five minutes. What just happened? What happened before that? Was there any cause-effect in that process?" When you get back to the point where lack of respect reared its ugly head, you can ask, "Do you see what happened here? What did that do to our group?" If you use this approach, you have to be careful not to assign blame or to allow youth to blame someone else for causing the problem in the first place.

Another model for teaching respect in verbal disagreements is helping youth understand the issue. If Mark disagrees with Anna, he has to restate what Anna said before he can state his disagreement. The leader then checks with Anna to see if that is what she said (meant). Sometimes this will clear up the disagreement, simply because a statement has been misunderstood. At the least, this process will lower the risk of tempers getting out of control, because we have pushed people to understand one another in the process of disagreement. Since we are talking about teaching respect by example, it is important that leaders model this process when they disagree with youth.

Here is still another model. Many youth protect themselves against lack of respect by prefacing what they want to say with phrases such as these: "This may sound stupid, but..." or "I know this is a silly question, but..." Whenever you hear this, you can model respect by saying

24

something such as, "There is no such thing as a stupid question if you really want to know the answer" or "I understand you think it may sound stupid, but it was an interesting way of getting at the question." Always affirm what people say, even if it is out of left field. The important thing is not correcting misinformation but affirming people. You can always correct misinformation after the affirmation: "Alex, thank you for that idea. You have suggested a creative way of dealing with the issue. Unfortunately, you may not have been aware of these realities." Then you can lay out the correct information.

Dealing With Discipline

How do we begin to establish community rules?

12 Begin with your leadership team and/or your youth ministry council. Talk about why you need community rules and what those rules might look like. Most rules of conduct are written while planning for a trip away from the church: How are youth—and adults—expected to behave away from home? Most rules are described as covenants of conduct, agreements that all participants are expected to sign and live up to. What should be included in covenants of conduct? As a minimum, you should include expectations about behavior: smoking, alcohol, drugs, inappropriate sexual behavior, and so forth. Be clear about what the expectation is. If you mean absolutely no smoking, you should say so. Remind adults that they will be held to the same set of expectations. Spell out the consequences of violating the covenant.

Then write up your covenant of conduct in a systematic form. Provide space for youth to sign, indicating that they have read the covenant and agree to abide by it. Also provide a space for parents to sign, indicating that they have read the covenant, support it, and will support you if you have to invoke consequences on their child. Adult counselors and other volunteers should also sign the covenant, indicating that they will abide by it.

13 **What are some guidelines for enforcing a covenant of conduct? How do we handle a youth who will not honor the commitments made to the group?**

Guidelines should be written into the covenant, spelled out clearly and in detail. For example, any indication of drug use will result in the person being sent home on the first available transportation, at the parent's expense. Be sure youth understand the covenant and know you are serious about the consequences. Then you have to carry through. The hard part will be when a person violates the covenant and you want to show grace and forgiveness by giving a second chance. If the covenant says zero tolerance, then the only way to show grace is to enforce the consequences. To take a minor example, we were on a conference mission tour when one of the youth began having serious medical problems. A trip to the doctor revealed that she had not told us everything she should have on the medical forms submitted with the application for the trip. This could have been life-threatening. She was not supposed to lift anything, but she had been helping with a service project. I told her that if she lifted anything heavier than her plate the rest of the trip, she would be on the first train home. She lived up to that commitment and expectation, and the rest of the group was willing to help carry her suitcase. A more serious example is the youth director who had two busloads of senior highs on the way to a ski trip when he discovered a youth smoking marijuana. The youth director called the youth's parents, told them the youth would be on such-and-such a flight, and they should plan to meet the flight. They were told why the youth was coming home, and they agreed that the youth director had made the right decision. Other youth leaders who were in a work camp or retreat setting closer to home have called parents to come get youth who were being disruptive and/or violating the covenant.

14 **At what point do we turn on the tough love?**

The short form of the answer is, You turn on the tough love whenever

- the covenant is violated,
- youth need to be protected,
- adults need to be protected.

15 How do we deal with youth who provoke the question, Why are you here?

A teacher took over a senior high Sunday school class where the youth were anything but cooperative or interested. After about three months, the teacher discovered that the youth were pleased that they had run off teachers each of the past five years. That teacher handled the situation by ignoring the fact that the class did not want her and was trying to run her off. She kept right on teaching. That was tough to do some Sundays because the group refused to discuss anything. But she continued to be there, continued to like the youth, and continued to try to draw them out. It was a rough year, but some of those youth later apologized and became strong leaders of the class the next year.

That is the only way I know for dealing with youth like that. Whether it is one person or an entire class, ignore the fact that they do not want you. Keep on teaching and trying to draw them out. And never stop loving them. Hey, nobody said it was easy.

16 What do we say to youth who stay away because other youth are so disruptive?

And, of course, the youth who stay away are the ones you most want in your group. If it is a fellowship group, this may be the time to organize a separate Bible study or covenant group—by invitation only. This will allow you to work with the youth who are serious about learning and growing in faith on a deeper level. It will also allow you to continue working with the disruptive youth in the fellowship setting, gently leading them to want to grow in faith.

If the situation is a Sunday school class, ask the youth who are staying away if they would be willing to come back and help you rebuild the group on a more solid basis. Commit to cracking down on the disruptions. Some youth who are staying away will be more willing to come back if they see you are making an effort to deal with disruptive youth.

In every case, let youth who are staying away know that you understand the problem. Invite them to help you think about ways in which you could help them grow in faith in another setting. Or invite them to help you deal with the problem directly. Positive peer pressure can be an important factor in dealing with disruptions.

17 How do we reach youth who are more focused on entertaining their peers than on what is happening in the class/fellowship group?

The question assumes that you want to reach (engage) these youth, rather than just control them. Here are some suggestions that might work singly or in combination. Go out of your way to relate to these youth outside the group. Find out *why* they are focused the way they are. They may have some serious issues (such as not feeling loved, feeling no one cares, feeling excluded) that explain their behavior and that you can address as a significant part of your ministry.

If there are no issues beyond entertainment, then you are probably dealing with a problem of lack of maturity. In this case, turn the tables on them. Work hard to find some learning activities, such as roleplay, where these youth can be entertaining and still be a part of the learning process.

If all else fails, you may simply have to say, "I love you, but I won't tolerate that kind of behavior." Then make that stick. You cannot allow a handful of youth to destroy the group with their entertainment needs.

18 How do we maintain a semblance of order without yelling, threatening, or punishing?

One way is to simply ignore a certain amount of disorder. After all, some disorder is nothing more than high-energy youth who are being asked to focus on one thing. Decide in advance how much disorder you will tolerate and what you will do when your point of no toleration has been reached.

So, what do you do when your point of no toleration has been reached? One strategy is to ask questions: Who can tell me what has happened in the past three minutes? Is what we're doing a way of showing love for one another? How would you feel if you were the leader of this group? This could lead to a healthy discussion, which would be a distraction from the point of the session; but, hey, you are already distracted. What do you have to lose?

A second strategy is to be silent. A respected youth leader can simply sit quietly, not doing anything but watching the group. In a few minutes, youth will begin to be uncomfortable with the silence and begin to quiet themselves down. Some youth will take leadership at this point and bring the group under control themselves. An alternative to silence is a few seconds of silence on your part, followed by your softly singing a song that

30

is a signal to quiet down and focus. You will usually not have to sing more than two choruses before the group catches on and begins to join in. When everyone is singing, you can return to the session.

A third strategy is called rebuke with affirmation: I love you, Jessica, but I won't tolerate that kind of behavior. Matt, I appreciate your enthusiasm for your school winning the big game, but we need to put that behind us for now. Sarah, you have a real gift for friendship, but we need to stop the side conversations.

Sometimes, of course, all other things fail, and we have to take action. I confess that I once expelled four junior high boys from youth group for a month because of their disruptive behavior. Fortunately, their parents backed me up, and those boys straightened out and became leaders in the group and my good friends.

How do we get their attention to start the meeting?

19

Well, you can always yell loud enough to be heard over the noise of the group. But that sets a tone for the meeting that suggests the loudest voice gets to set the agenda. I prefer a quieter approach. Whenever it is time to settle down, drop the conversations, and begin the meeting (or class), I sing "Sanctuary" as many times as I need to in order to get their attention. The first time I tried it, I had to sing the chorus four times. After a few weeks, the group was singing along before I reached the end the first time.

Topics/ Resources

In almost every workshop I have ever led, the first questions had to do with topics and resources. Where do I find good resources that will keep youth involved? What resource should I use for confirmation (or for Sunday school)? In every workshop, I dealt with that question the same way: "We are not ready for that yet. You first have to know why you want resources. What is it that you want to do in Christian education with youth (either Sunday morning, Sunday evening, or any other setting) that requires resources?" This response frustrated a lot of groups, but it did focus on the real issue. You see, if you do not know where you want to go, any resource will get you there. So, you first have to have a road map, a game plan, a strategy for youth ministry. Then you have an idea of the kinds of resources you need to help you work out your game plan.

20 Where do we find new approaches and/or ideas for topics/resources?

Start with your own game plan (master plan or road map): What is it that you want to do in youth ministry? What are key issues for you and your youth? What is it that you are looking for in a resource, or in a list of topics? When you have that game plan firmly in mind, you can begin looking for new ideas and approaches.

33

But why wait? Why not start off by looking for new ideas/approaches and build your plan around them? Because that strategy begins with a resource or an idea and not with the needs of your youth and the long-range strategies you have developed for meeting those needs. You may find a new idea on the Internet and rush it right into your youth program, only to discover that it does not come close to meeting the spiritual needs of your youth. Plus, there are not that many new ideas and/or approaches out there, so most of the ideas have been used in the history of Christian education. You can find some new ways to use old approaches/ideas, because technology and other equipment developments give you new tools. But the ideas are pretty much the same.

Now, having said all that, you still need some freshness in what you are doing. So, let's assume that you have a serious game plan and are not looking for a magic answer to all your problems. Where can you find some new approaches and ideas?

- Check out the Web for some helpful resources. See the list of websites in this book (pages 119–20) that other youth workers have found helpful.
- Take a new look at existing resources. Keep a library of resources from more than one publisher, and hang onto old copies of resources. Can you take a method from one resource and use it to teach content from a second resource? For example, Resource A has great content about a tough Bible passage, but its teaching-learning method is read and discuss. Resource B has incredibly shallow content for teaching a Bible passage, but the teaching-learning method is interactive, involves more than one way of learning (see Questions 22 and 94), and sounds as if it would be appealing to youth. This approach takes some serious work on your part, but the payoff is tremendous.
- Where do you find new topics for discussion, particularly in the areas of decision making and current issues? One place is daily newspapers or newsmagazines. Another is electronic resources, such as LinC (see www.ileadyouth.com, on page 120). Talk to youth to find out what national and international issues are engaging their attention. Talk with other youth leaders, both in your community and on the Web. All kinds of topics are floating around. Check out the ones that fit both the needs of your group and the game plan you have developed for Christian education with youth.

What makes a resource good?

Here is the answer everyone hates: It depends on what you want the resource to do. If you do not know what you want to do, or where you want to go, any resource will get you there (see Questions 20, 28, 30, 94, and 95). Once you know what you want to do, you can choose your resource accordingly.

Having said that, here are some general guidelines for what makes a resource good. A good resource

- has an inner integrity; that is, there is a coherence and plan about the resource. It has clear objectives and a clear plan for reaching those objectives.
- takes into account the various ways youth learn (see Questions 22 and 94).
- has clear, easily understood directions for leaders.
- offers the opportunity for at least some degree of in-depth probing of the topic and for dealing with related questions not covered by the session plan.
- fits your goals and objectives. This means that no single resource will be good for all groups and all situations. Rather, the definition of good depends on what you need for your own ministry. Fortunately for religious publishers, there are enough similar needs and game plans that developing resources can still be profitable.

The preceding list assumes a structured learning setting, such as Sunday school or a Bible study. Resources for fellowship groups should also offer much the same benefits, although in perhaps a less-structured form.

How do we choose resources that meet the needs of everyone?

Again, the answer is not popular, since it does not involve a magic wand and does involve some preparation and forethought on the part of your leadership team: No single resource is going to meet the needs of all the youth in your group all the time. So, what do you do?

First, be clear about what you perceive the needs of your youth to be. Where are they in their spiritual journeys? What foundational studies do they need to have a firm basis for their growth in faith? Where are their interests? What is their age level? What is their level of maturity?

Second, be aware that not all youth prefer to learn in the same way, so you will need different resources to meet their needs in learning preferences (see Question 94). If youth never have the opportunity to learn in the way that is most comfortable to them, they will begin to drop out. But if they recognize that, on a fairly regular basis (not necessarily every Sunday), they can learn in the way they most prefer, they will become more deeply involved. This is meeting youth needs on a serious level. So, look for resources that are tuned into using a variety of learning methods.

Look at resources to see which fit the needs of your youth. Which resources offer a variety of topics to involve youth in growth in faith? Which resources offer a variety of teaching-learning activities so that you can offer youth the chance to learn in the way they most prefer? Remember that not every activity, or even every session, will speak to all the ways in which youth prefer to learn. After all, people prefer to learn in a wide variety of ways.

23 How in-depth should we go in Bible study with youth?

Go as far as youth want to go. If they want to dig into historical background, geography, and social customs, help them find resources and turn them loose. (*The Interpreter's Dictionary of the Bible, The Oxford Companion to the Bible,* and a good Bible atlas are the basic resources you need for this. You should be able to find all of them in your pastor's library, the church library, or the public library.) If you feel inadequate to deal with their questions and concerns, step right up and say so. Then tell them you will help them find the resources they need and will work with them to discover the answers. Plan for some kind of result from their study that they can show off. Maybe they can make a map of Abraham's journeys or a chronological table of the period from Moses to David. Or they could put together a newspaper that headlines the biblical story and has supporting columns that cover all the background information.

If the in-depth information your youth want has to do with the way the Bible applies to life, rather than to background, that is also good. You may still want to push them to do some work on biblical background so that they understand something about the social context in which a passage was written. As they talk about implications of a passage, also be sure they understand the context in the Bible. Taking a sentence or paragraph out of context can completely change the implications of its

36

meaning. Again, if you feel out of your depth, say so and commit to working together on understanding a passage. Use commentaries, Bible handbooks, and other resources to help you think about the implications of a passage.

24. What topics should we avoid in dealing with youth?

Do not avoid any topic in which youth have a real interest. As you plan to deal with controversial topics, you need to be aware of possible parental and congregational reactions. Talk with the pastor and with key parents, and explain what you are going to be talking about and the context in which you will be doing it. One of the advantages of a long-range plan (see Questions 28 and 95) is that parents should already know the context in which learning for youth will be taking place. This gives them a sense of security when controversial topics come up; they have some assurance that you are not going off the deep end just to keep youth interested but will deal with controversial topics in a biblical and theological framework that fits within the stance of your denomination.

25. Topics about sexuality are often ignored by the church. How can we carefully and responsibly deal with them?

This question points up several key issues. First, the church often ignores this topic because we have difficulty in talking about human sexuality. Second, when we deal with sexuality, we need to do it carefully and responsibly, since the church has so much trouble talking about sexuality. Anytime there is a potential flashpoint in dealing with a topic, we need to be doubly careful and responsible about planning and presentation.

Having said that, how do we go about talking about sexuality? Begin by pulling together a planning team that includes, in some capacity, the pastor, the youth leaders, parents, and some youth. You want to build as broad a base of support as possible early in the planning. The planning team should outline purposes and goals for dealing with sexuality, possible topics, and potential resources in the community. You may need to push the planning team to include some topics that are more controversial, such as safe sex and homosexuality. Certainly, you want to push them to move beyond "Just say no" as a moral guideline. Values and decision making should be key elements in any programs on sexuality. Continue to check your goals against the Social Principles, which are in

37

The Book of Discipline of The United Methodist Church, so that you are sure you are working within parameters established by The United Methodist Church. (Or refer to similar guidelines for other denominations.)

What about resources? First, check denominational sources to see what kinds of print and video resources are offered for use in the local church. Then check with the conference youth director to see if there are trained teams in the conference who can offer special sexuality seminars in your local church. Are there potential leaders in your area, such as hospital training and outreach programs, social services, and so forth? Who are potential leaders for talking about values in sexuality, as well as decision making? What guides of resources are available to help those leaders prepare and lead sessions?

Then you will want your planning team to decide how to promote the sessions. Will they be advertised widely? Will you open the sessions to all youth in your community? How will you spread the word? How will you deal with church members who complain that the church should not be involved in that kind of teaching (or who want you to promote only simplistic responses to complex issues)?

Questions You Didn't Ask

26

What should I look for as I evaluate resources?

Resources convey both implicit and explicit messages. Some resources may appear appropriate on the surface, but you discover, as you look deeper, that the implicit messages are not consistent with the theology and values of your youth program and may actually contradict the explicit messages of the resource. As you evaluate resources, consider these things:

- What does this resource imply about the nature of God?
- What images of God are portrayed in this resource?
- How does this resource depict other cultures and races?
- Do the activities in this resource exclude people with disabilities from being able to participate?
- Does this resource reinforce ethnic- or gender-based stereotypes?
- Do the examples and activities assume that everyone comes from an upper-middle class economic bracket?
- How is the Bible used in this resource?

- Does this resource encourage youth to use in their own lives what they are learning?
- Are the suggested activities appropriate for the mental, social, and spiritual level of maturity of your youth?
- Do the suggested activities create a situation where there will be winners and losers?
- Do the suggested activities create a situation where a youth may feel put down for his or her ideas?

Long-Range Planning and Youth Ownership

How do we plan long-range?

27 Questions 28 and 92 address the issue of developing a game plan for youth ministry. We will look at the related question of planning long-range for specific events and programs/activities. The assumption is that you have already set some long-range goals; you have an answer to the question, What do we want youth to learn, experience, and do from the time they enter youth ministry until they graduate, in order for them to grow in faith and discipleship? As you plan, look ahead to see what national, conference, and district youth events are scheduled in the next year or two. These events can become pegs on which to hang your planning. Remember to block out time for mission trips, work camps, and other service activities, as well as camping, canoe trips, and so forth.

Planning for specific events or programs/activities becomes an intermediate step in reaching your long-range goals. For major events, such as a national youth event, a mission trip, and similar activities, begin planning a year ahead. Here are some steps to follow in your long-range planning:

- Begin publicity with your youth group and congregation. Let them know about the event, what it is, and how attending it will benefit them.
- Gather registrations for the event. If you are planning a trip where you work out your own housing along the way, begin working with local churches to arrange for your youth group to sleep in their basements.

41

- Work on fundraising for the trip. National youth events, mission trips, and work camps are more expensive than short trips around the local area or conference and district events. Begin planning early for fundraising so that you do not have to focus on this at the last minute and overwhelm both the youth and the congregation with too many fundraisers too close together.
- Work out your travel plans. Does the church have a van? Have you reserved it well in advance? Or does the conference or district have a bus going to a national event? Do you need to charter a bus for a major trip? Can you depend on parents to help provide transportation?

It is also important to plan ahead for local programs and activities, although you may not have to begin planning as far ahead as for national events. Let's assume, for purposes of illustration, that you want to begin a Bible study for older youth who are beginning to drop out of the youth program. Here are some things you need to consider:

- Why do you want to begin a Bible study? What will be the hook for this Bible study that will make it unique and cause older youth to want to attend?
- Who will be the target audience for the study? If the target audience is older youth, you will plan the content and approach differently from the way you would plan for junior highs (see Question 42).
- What will be the content of the study? What resources are available for such a study?
- Who will lead the study?
- How will you promote the group with your older youth? Simply putting a notice in the church bulletin will not draw the people you most want. You will need to promote and recruit: write letters and e-mails, make phone calls, talk to youth personally whenever you happen to run into them.
- How will you maintain the group? This is a key question we often ignore in our long-range planning. We start a new group with a lot of excitement and hope and then expect it to continue on its own momentum. Groups, particularly new groups with an audience as fragile as older youth, need a lot of nurture and maintenance. How will you plan to build on the enthusiasm of the beginning to keep the group alive and growing?

28 How do we work out a plan but still give youth ownership and get them involved?

The question assumes that long-range planning is primarily the work of adult leaders. This is, in my view, a correct assumption. Adult leadership will provide the continuity and vision for long-range planning in youth ministry. The question also assumes that youth need to be involved in planning so that they have ownership in what happens. So, the question really means, How do we balance the two so that youth have ownership and we have a coherent long-range plan?

Begin by having youth represented on the planning team. This does not have to be a lot of youth but enough so that youth concerns can be heard. After all, youth know a lot about who they are, what their life is like, and what questions and concerns they have. This does not mean that youth are allowed to dictate everything that happens, simply that they have a voice in developing the plan.

Then, at intervals, take the plan in progress to a youth meeting and say, "Here's where we think we're going, and here's why we think we're going there. How does that sound to you?" Again, the idea is not to have an up-or-down vote but to get responses, suggestions, and ideas from the total youth group. This broadens the base of ownership and makes it more likely that the plan will be successful when you put it into practice—*if*, of course, you really listen to what the youth are saying and take their concerns seriously. That does not mean you have to adopt every suggestion they make. It does mean youth need to know that you are taking them seriously and that they will be able to see some of what they suggest in the final plan.

As a part of the planning process, offer youth choices. Choices always have parameters. Do not ask, "What would you like to study?" Ask instead, "As a part of dealing with decision making, would you prefer we consider issues about science and ethics, or ethics in public life?" This gives youth a choice, within parameters. The key is that planners will have a goal in mind that, in this case, deals with ethics and decision making. The learning goals are the same for either forum. Youth have a real choice, but it is within a framework that fits a long-range plan.

29 How much planning is too much to give over to youth themselves?

It depends. (Don't you love that straight-forward, decisive answer?) It depends, first of all, on the group itself. How mature are the youth? How willing are they to work hard at planning and to take seriously all the things that go into developing a game plan for youth ministry? A small church with a youth group of about fifteen relied on youth for planning all the programs for fellowship group. The youth decided at the beginning of the year what topics they wanted to deal with on Sunday evenings. They worked out how many Sundays they would spend on each topic and what part of the topic each Sunday would cover. Then each Sunday was assigned to a specific youth, who prepared and led the program for the evening. Youth who are incredibly busy probably do not have time for that depth of involvement. But they would probably be willing to help develop a list of questions that youth are asking, or to make decisions about what content, values, and experiences would help them probe a part of the game plan.

Because you want to plan long-range, and youth graduate and move on, ultimate control of the planning process needs to stay in the leadership team. But youth can be involved in that process, as we have seen in both this question and in the previous one. Give youth responsibility in small doses, for specific areas, as a part of the total planning process in the leadership team. As youth gain skills and confidence in planning, give them additional responsibility as they are willing to accept it. Include younger youth in the planning process so that they can gain skills and confidence in planning for ministry. Include as a part of the plan for younger youth specific units on planning and decision making. Teach them how to plan by allowing them to help make decisions for a retreat or some other activity.

30 How can youth be encouraged to plan their own ministries?

You can encourage them by giving them specific responsibilities in planning. Do this in small steps so that they can succeed and gain confidence in the process. Do not begin by saying, "The fall retreat is coming up. What do you want to do?" Rather, say something such as, "The fall retreat is coming up. I'd like for you to think about the times for worship at the retreat and suggest some ways we can make them more meaningful. First, let's talk about last year. What was there about the worship that really spoke to you?" Then you can move the group to explore what it is about worship that speaks to them, what kinds of experiences are meaningful, and so forth. They may suggest a Communion service or a time of baptismal renewal using the full ritual. (Yes, youth actually do say things like that. They love the mystery of ritual. It has a power that speaks to their souls.) Or they may suggest times of quiet meditation, where each person has thirty minutes to read the Bible and think about a specific question.

Invite them to think about the theme of the retreat, which should already be decided. Of the kinds of worship they have listed, which ones would lend themselves to carrying out the theme? How would they do that?

Then invite youth to help you think about specifics. What kind of worship experience would go at what time during the retreat? What equipment and supplies will be needed for that? Who will take responsibility for gathering supplies and preparing the worship space? Who will help lead the worship time?

This model can be used for planning all kinds of activities and programs, each of which speaks to specific youth needs—because youth have been involved in the planning. In the real world of the twenty-first century, most youth are so busy that they will not be able to give a lot of time to planning, so you may need to include planning times as part of your fellowship time on Sunday evenings (or whenever you have it).

31 We need help in planning for long-range projects, specifically setting priorities (Why do youth want to go?) and planning and logistics (What do we do about fundraising, making arrangements for the trip, and so forth?).

First, think about why youth want to go. Some will sign up for almost anything that looks fun. Some youth will sign up for a mission trip/work camp because they want to do something to help other people, to make a difference in the world, or to see a different part of the country. Some want to go to national events because they like the excitement of being part of a large group or because they want to hear outstanding speakers and musicians. The point is that different youth have different motivations, and you need to be aware of the differences so that you can appeal to all of them. You also need to be aware of what is appropriate in terms of motivation. For example, you do not promote a work camp, where youth are expected to spend long hours working on a project, the same way you promote a rock concert. You do not promote a backpacking or canoeing trip—where you will be camping out, doing lots of physical exertion, and expecting everyone to take an equal share of responsibility—the same way you promote a national youth event.

Involve youth in planning and promotion. If youth know what the event is, they know how to promote it to their friends in a way that will be both honest and appealing. They also know how to apply tough love: "John, you may want to think a long time before you sign up for this trip. It requires a lot of hard work—and getting up early. It will be fun, but not party-time fun. Think it over carefully." Involving youth in planning helps motivate them for the details of the trip, including getting registration, money, medical forms, and permission slips in on time. It also prepares them for the less attractive parts of the trip, such as long hours in a van, sleeping on church basement floors, working hard in the heat, and not having access to unlimited hot water, telephones, and e-mail.

Now, think about the planning. Plan in reverse order; that is, put down the date for the event or trip and then work backward from there. List all the things you need to do in order to make the trip a success. Then list when each of those things needs to be done. As a final step, you may want to put down a date for when you need to start working on each of the steps, just so you will not get caught at the last minute. The chart below is one way to illustrate what we mean.

YOUTH MISSION TRIP

Task	Begin Work	Task Completed
Publicity and recruiting	December 1	January 15
Fundraising	February 15	June 1
Youth registration drive	February 15	March 15
Arrange transportation	March 15	May 15
Arrange housing	April 15	June 1
All permission forms in	May 1	June 30
Medical forms in	May 1	June 30

Trip: July 6–16

Some of that may seem early, but it is much better to be early than to be late. In the case of transportation, for example, if you are competing with other groups for the use of the church van, you need to be on the list early. If you need to charter a bus, you may need to begin looking for bids

46

even earlier. The same is true for planning fundraising for the trip. You want to be on the church calendar early so that you are not competing with a lot of other events for people's time and attention. Also, this planning schedule takes place during Lent and Easter, when most churches have extra activities that you need to plan around.

Early registration is also important. You may have youth who have to cancel and other youth who decide later they would like to go, but those details can be worked out. People who register early save money for national (and some conference) youth events. Since those events also require cash deposits, you need to plan for early fundraising, or borrow from your youth budget until the fundraising phase is complete.

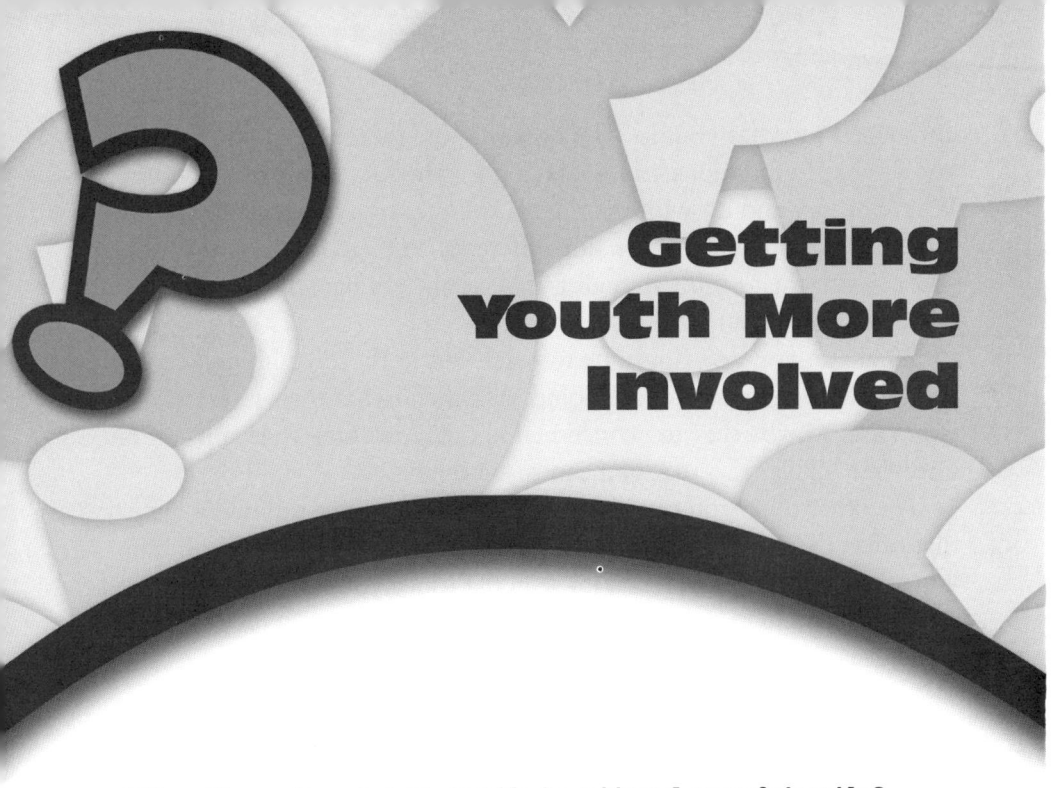

Getting Youth More Involved

How do we get youth to attend consistently?

32 The word *consistently* seems to recognize the reality that every youth is not going to attend every session, whether it is Sunday school or a fellowship group. Given that reality, the best way to get youth to attend consistently is to have

- a sense of belonging to the group;
- a welcoming atmosphere for newcomers;
- quality lessons/programs;
- trained, caring leaders/teachers;
- consistent follow-up when youth miss.

All of those together will not guarantee youth will attend consistently, but building on them will put you ahead of the curve on that issue.

How do we draw into the faith those youth who are on the outside/fringe of the group? Some of them come regularly but do not seem to be touched by what we do.

33 My passion in youth ministry has always been drawing youth into the faith and helping them grow in faith and understanding. In the real world, some youth will come but will always be on the fringes and seem

49

untouched by what you do. The hopeful note there is that you do not know what foundations you are laying for the future in those youth. What you say and do with them now, even though they do not seem touched by it, may make a major difference to them in the future. What you do with them, futile though it may seem, is a part of God's work of prevenient grace in their lives.

What can you do? Continue to reach out to those youth and try to include them in what you are doing. Ask them what their interests and issues are. Maybe they are concerned about something that you can build into your ministry so that you can reach them.

The other thing you can do is not give up. Continue to build a ministry that offers the opportunity for a maturing faith. Pray that God will give you a handle on how to reach those in the fringe youth. Trust God to bless what you do and to work in their lives. Remember that God's prevenient grace does work, and your ministry is one instrument of that grace.

34 We have good attendance at social events, but it is like pulling teeth to get youth involved with mission projects and fundraisers. Help!

Part of the issue may be motivation. How do you approach publicity/recruiting for mission projects and fundraisers? With the schedules youth keep these days, they need to know how participating in a project will pay off for them. One question that is always in the back of their minds is, What's in it for me? Keep that in mind as you plan for mission projects.

Another way to get them involved is to take a small group on a mission/work project, even if you do not have quite enough youth to do all the tasks involved. Work extra hard to be sure the trip/project is a success—that is, that youth have a good time, that they see that they make a difference, and that they make the connection between the project and their growing faith (the "What does this have to do with God?" question). These youth then become your best salespeople for the next event. And, if youth get fired up about a mission trip/work camp, it is reasonable to them that they need to have fundraisers so that they can afford to make the trip. (See Question 45 for other suggestions related to this question.)

35 How do we deal with the fact that youth have such incredibly busy schedules and we want them to commit even more time and energy?

Good question. I have seen the calendars my youth carry, and every daily page is full. There are at least two issues here. One is a pastoral issue: How do we protect youth who are already too busy and not getting enough rest? The other is a ministry issue: We have something to offer youth that they do not get anywhere else, and we ought not be embarrassed about offering it. How do we hold the two issues in some kind of creative balance?

We need to be honest with our youth on two fronts. First, we need to let them know that we are aware that they are already too busy and do not have a lot of discretionary time. Second, we need to let them know how important we think the ministry/maturing faith issues are. Then we need to talk about making decisions: If you cannot do everything, and almost everything you want to do is good (so that you are not asking them to choose between good stuff and bad stuff), how do you set priorities? An important part of your ministry could be an annual workshop of how to set priorities for time and energy, how to make decisions, and how to live out those decisions when crunch time comes on the schedule.

Also, provide a wide menu of choices, and be sure youth understand that you do not expect every youth to participate in every activity. Then you have to discipline yourself not to push the key youth to be involved in everything. After all, if the key youth are not involved in an activity, that gives someone else a chance to develop leadership skills.

But what do you do if you are in a small-membership church that has to have almost every youth involved in every activity so that you will have a critical mass to make things happen? Well, you have a couple things going for you. With a small number of youth, you can have all the youth involved in making decisions about which programs and activities to offer. This makes it easier for youth to commit their time to those programs and activities. The other thing you have going for you is that you do not have to offer as wide a spread of activities in a smaller group, which means you can focus on fewer things (in terms of preparation). And youth can focus on a smaller number of activities and give themselves more freely.

Build sabbath time into your program. Sabbath, here, does not mean a day of rest but regularly scheduled opportunities for youth to be quiet; to reflect, in the light of faith, on issues of importance to them; and to build some stability into their lives. This accomplishes two things at once. It allows you to program activities for youth that actually help them deal with the stresses of their life while increasing their participation in the life of the church.

36. I attend a commuter church. How do we get community youth involved in the church? What is a good start?

A good start is a firm commitment from adult leaders in the congregation. Be sure they know what it is they are committing to. For example, they may be excited about your wanting to involve community youth, but they may not want any extra wear and tear on the building or any of the "wrong" kids coming to the church. Be clear about what you intend to do, why you want to do it, and what your target audience is. It is much better to spend extra time on this in the beginning than to begin reaching community youth and then discover that the church's leaders are not willing to support a ministry to "those people." (Sorry, but that happens in the real world.)

But, let's say you have all the support you need, including money and adult volunteers. How do you reach neighborhood youth? Some churches do this by sponsoring basketball or volleyball nights, either in the church gym or on the parking lot. Recently, I talked with a pastor whose church has a dance for middle-high kids (grades six through eight) on a regular basis. This has been so successful that they have had to turn youth away (because of fire codes on the number of people allowed in the gym).

Whatever the activity is, your first step has to be something that will be attractive to unchurched youth and give you a chance to begin to get acquainted with youth in the community. Spend a lot of time talking to the youth before and after basketball games, during a dance, or whatever it is you do to attract them. Begin to connect names and faces and to pick up on needs in the community. Youth may need tutoring or a safe place to hang out after school one or two evenings a week. Be alert for them to ask the inevitable question, "How come you're doing this for us?" That is your foot in the door to witness. Do not jump in and give them the whole load the first time; tell them about God's incredible love,

52

which you are trying to share with the community. This is also your entry point for talking to them about faith. Lay the groundwork for developing faith groups by inviting them to worship, Sunday school, and youth group. Lay the groundwork within existing groups so that the groups will be welcoming to neighborhood youth (and, eventually, to their families). You are working on two fronts here. One is reaching out to the community and inviting people into the church. The other is working within the church to be sure that neighborhood youth will be welcomed and the programs will be attractive enough that they will want to come back a second time.

37 How do we keep more-mature junior highs interested in coming back when less-mature youth dominate the group?

This is a major issue. In general, junior high girls are more mature than junior high boys are, at least socially. Work on community building as a part of your curriculum (see Questions 1–11), and build in a variety of learning activities (see Questions 22 and 94). From time to time, divide youth into smaller groups for short discussion times. Sometimes allow the more-mature youth to form their own groups, which will allow them to function at a more-mature level. Remember that the most-mature junior highs will act in immature ways at times. Girls will be as restless and silly as boys. So, providing for the needs of more-mature youth is not a total either/or situation.

38 What are some ways to focus seventh and eighth graders on serious issues?

Vary the presentation of the materials. Serious issues can be presented in ways that are attractive to younger adolescents and still be serious. Younger adolescents are not ready developmentally to sit still and read and discuss all the time. Use more-active ways of learning, such as games, roleplays, and simulations; and try to make learning as experiential and interactive as possible.

Take into account differences in preferred ways of learning (see Questions 22 and 94). If the resources you are using do not offer a variety of teaching/learning styles, consider looking for other resources. And remember that art and music are teaching/learning methods.

39 How do we hold the attention of seventh and eighth graders for an hour's worth of serious material?

Realistically, you probably do not hold their attention. Your best chance is to do some active learning, have a variety of teaching/learning activities, and shift activities every five minutes or so. A variety of resources are available to help you do this. See the resources for this section in "For Further Reading" (pages 122–123).

40 We live in a small town and have only a few youth. With so few, it is hard to do some things. What can we do?

It is tough hearing about all the wonderful things youth groups in megachurches are doing and knowing that all your small-town church can do is be envious. But you also have some strengths in your small group. First, you have a built-in community, which can be nurtured and built up (see Questions 1–11). You can put the whole group in one van and have a great time of fellowship and even of learning as you travel to district/conference events, to a park for a picnic, or to wherever you are going. Second, your logistical problems are easier to manage. Third, you likely have a much higher percentage of youth in attendance than the large churches have. The youth in your church know they have to be there if the group is going to work, and they are willing to take on that responsibility. Fourth, it is easier to involve the entire group in planning.

So, even though you have those advantages, are there some creative things you can do? One possibility is to pair up for some events with a church of the same denomination in a neighboring town, or with a church of another denomination in your own town. This could give you the critical mass of youth you need for a retreat, a work camp or mission project, or a fun trip.

Another possibility is to plug into district and conference youth events, which are well attended by youth from groups the size of yours. One of the pitfalls of some large youth groups is that they often do not go to events beyond the local church, since they are self-sustaining and have enough youth to do whatever they want. Send youth to church camp and take them to district youth rallies and institutes, as these connections help them feel part of something bigger than themselves. Connection is a powerful tool; it is also a source of inspiration, new ideas, and enthusiasm for another year.

54

41 We live in a small town where most of the youth go to another church. Our few youth get discouraged because the other church's programming looks so exciting. What can we do?

First, look at your long-range plan. Remind yourself what you want to accomplish through your youth ministry. Look for gaps in your long-range plan, and then build a specialized youth ministry to plug those gaps. For example, if you discover you are weak on spiritual formation, you can design ways of helping your youth grow spiritually (see Questions 43–51). An annual spiritual life retreat, in addition to what you do in the local church setting, can be a big boost to your youth's morale. Plan for programs/learnings focused on your denominational heritage: Where did you come from? What does your denomination believe? What is the heritage of your local church? Dealing with the question about your church's history is a great way to get older adults involved in youth ministry, as they know the stories and the reasons your church does some of the things it does. Send youth out with lists of questions and tape recorders to get those stories. Then work with other adults to get the stories on paper and into some kind of printed form to share with the whole congregation. The local newspaper editor, an English teacher, or a professional writer in your community could work with the youth on this project. It could really pay off for your youth if you teach them to be *United Methodist* Christians.

Questions You Didn't Ask

42 How do we work with age-level differences?

Another reality about youth is that, as they mature physically and socially, there are crucial differences between (and even within) age levels in terms of interest, learning preferences, and so forth. We all know that there are vast differences between seventh graders and twelfth graders. We recognize that there are smaller, but still significant, differences between seventh graders and ninth graders, or between ninth graders and twelfth graders. For example, older youth are more likely to raise questions and to test out new ideas than are younger youth. Older youth have more developmental capacity for synthesizing information and spotting critical issues. Younger youth have more difficulty in sitting still. They also think more concretely and, to some extent, compartmentalize information.

Another difference is in faith styles. Younger adolescents are interested in issues of belonging, while older adolescents are into questioning. One model for how this plays out is seen in recent proposals for a multitiered approach to confirmation. For younger adolescents, the focus in confirmation would be on belonging issues: What does it mean to belong to the church? What are the secret words and handshakes that make you a Christian? Other important components of belonging are knowing the creeds, the Lord's Prayer, and other elements commonly used in worship and participating in worship, prayer, and stewardship. Another key element for confirmation with younger adolescents is the history and teachings of the denomination: What does it mean to be United Methodist? What is unique about who we are? Where did we come from? What is our heritage? Theology is important, but at a fairly basic level. For example, it is not crucial for sixth or seventh graders to dig into the mystery of the Trinity. For older youth, theology becomes the focus, since they tend to question everything. The same youth with whom you worked on belonging in sixth or seventh grade, you now work with on theological/faith issues. At this point, you may want to deal not only with the Trinity but also with questions about the nature of God, who Jesus Christ is, the nature of salvation, the church, grace, social justice, the nature of the Bible. Doubt may be as important as faith in this process. For more details on faith styles and how they work out in Christian education with youth, see the books listed for this section in "For Further Reading" (pages 122–23).

Within age levels there are also crucial differences. In general, adolescent girls mature earlier than adolescent boys do. Once, when I was asked about the right age for confirmation, I said, tongue-in-cheek, that seventh-grade girls and twelfth-grade boys would be the right combination in terms of maturity levels. That is a bit of an exaggeration, but it points up what all of us who have ever tried to teach junior high Sunday school know to be a fact: Youth have major differences in social maturity, even though faith styles or learning developmental differences are not as wide.

If you are aware of the differences, and some of the potential problems the differences can cause, then you will be well on your way to dealing with the differences. Knowing the differences can also help you find the kinds of resources that will help you deal with the differences as you deal with serious issues of faith and life.

Balancing Spiritual Growth, Learning, and Fun

43

What does spiritual growth mean?

Youth workers will answer this question in a variety of ways. For some, it will mean being able to pray the Lord's Prayer and recite the Apostles' Creed. For some, it will mean always having an element of worship in youth activities. For some, it will mean intentionally leading youth to make commitments to Christ and the church. All of those can be important, depending on where your youth are.

For all groups, though, spiritual growth is closely related to faith maturity (see Question 51). This means that youth are growing in a vertical relationship with God through Jesus Christ and in a horizontal relationship of service with others. The Letter to the Ephesians says it like this: "…until all of us come to the unity of the faith and of the knowledge of the Son of God, to maturity, to the measure of the full stature of Christ" (Ephesians 4:13). Youth are not going to realize full maturity during adolescence; that would be an unrealistic expectation. However, they should begin to show signs of moving toward maturity.

Ministry with youth needs to include opportunities for them to grow toward maturity in their relationship with God. Does your worship invite them to relate with God through Jesus Christ? Do your study sessions help them grow in knowledge of God and of God's ways in the world? John Wesley referred to the way we work toward this dimension of spiritual growth as works of piety. They include

57

- prayer;
- Bible study;
- congregational worship;
- participation in the Lord's Supper;
- Christian conversation.

Do you include all of these elements in your youth ministry? By Christian conversation, Wesley meant being in a small group focused on growth in faith maturity and providing both support and the call to accountability. Do your conversations with one another, for example, offer opportunities for both support and calls to accountability? How often do you engage in prayer and Bible study? Do you encourage regular worship with the congregation? Or do you disparage that as big church and assume youth are not interested? Contemporary worship services for youth have their place, but not as a ministry that continues to isolate them from the congregation.

Ministry with youth needs to include opportunities for them to grow toward maturity in their relationships with other people and with the world. This horizontal growth toward maturity begins in youth group, Sunday school class, and local church and then reaches out toward the world. It includes fellowship, community, mission, and service. John Wesley often referred to these as works of mercy. They include
- feeding the hungry;
- clothing the naked;
- visiting the sick and those in prison;
- and responding in other ways to human need.

Do you include all these in your youth ministry? How often do you think about fellowship and community building as ways to mature in faith? How often do you provide opportunities for your youth to engage in direct, hands-on ministry with others? Do you do that regularly, or is service restricted to the annual mission trip? In addition, works of mercy sometimes involve moving to works of justice: actively working to change the system that allows people to be hungry, homeless, and in need in the first place.

Spiritual growth involves both works of piety and works of mercy. Prayer and Bible study lead us to minister to others. Ministry to others drives us back to prayer and Scripture for strength to go on with ministry to others.

44 The youth of our church are suspicious of anything labeled as Christian because they associate Christianity with the fundamentalism pervasive in the larger culture. They believe they know all about Christianity, when they actually know little. How can we share with them an authentic Christianity and not run them off?

One of the tragedies of the church in our time is that we have allowed fundamentalism to seize the agenda and define what the church is and believes. The tragedy lies in the reality that fundamentalism sees all issues as either–or and does not allow for diversity in opinion or action. One of the historic strengths of the church has been the freedom to disagree and work together in spite of disagreement. We air our differences together, work them out if possible, and continue to do God's mission in the world, even when we disagree.

For example, look at a current hot issue: Is it absolutely necessary to believe that abortion is murder in order to be a Christian? Can Christians honestly disagree on the moral and ethical issues about abortion and reproductive rights and still be Christian? Can they disagree and work together to feed the hungry, clothe the naked, and so forth? Can they disagree without reading one another out of the church?

Behind this question is the need for an alternative vision of what it means to be a Christian. How do we offer youth another way to love God and live their faith? One way, of course, is by personal example. If adult leaders are clearly Christian without being exclusive or dogmatic about their faith, they offer a model of an alternative to fundamentalism.

Another way to offer an alternative vision is programming. What if you met with a team of youth and adults and asked the question, "What is there about fundamentalism that turns us off so much? Is it an insistence of a literal interpretation of the Bible? Or is it the insistence that we believe certain things in order to be Christian? What is it?" Once you identify those issues, ask the team to help you identify how to engage youth in discussions about alternatives to fundamentalism. Engage your pastor in the conversation. He or she may be able to address some of the issues in preaching and definitely should be able to suggest resources and other background information for program building.

45 Where do we draw the line between wanting youth to enjoy coming to church and pushing them to grow beyond fellowship?

Two risks are implicit in this question. The first is the one we worry about the most: How can we help youth who come just for the fun to grow in faith? If we push them to grow in faith, will they quit coming? We certainly do not want to lose anyone. The second implicit risk is the opposite: If we cater to the youth who come only to have fun so that they will keep coming, will we lose the youth who want to grow in faith? The answer to the second question is probably yes.

So, where is the line, and how do we walk it? My personal bias is to risk losing the kids who come just for the fun so that we do not lose the ones we have a chance to help grow as disciples. But there are some ways we can accommodate both groups, up to a point.

Some of those youth who seem to be coming just for the fun can be enticed into growth without even being aware of it. Look for ways of learning and growing that will attract their attention. For example, one pastor who was dealing with this problem discovered that showing his slides of the Holy Land and talking about biblical events through that medium made youth who were there just for the fun want to know more about the Bible. Another adult worker with youth was trying to lead a Lenten session showing the parallels between Psalm 22 and Jesus' crucifixion. He stopped with Psalm 22:1, but one youth who had never shown any interest in the Bible before and was basically the group cut-up grabbed his Bible, read all of Psalm 22, and began to get excited about the parallels. The youth stopped the discussion, which was ready to move elsewhere, and gave a long report on what Psalm 22 said. (He was back to having fun the next week, but he was in a different place, anyway.)

Active learning is another way to engage youth who are there for the fun. They think they are in a game. Then, when it is time to reflect on the game and relate it to faith, they suddenly discover there is something more. Fellowship times that are strictly game nights draw lots of youth who do not seem to care about learning, but most of them will sit quietly for a closing worship time. Somewhere along the way, they are touched.

Youth who are pushing for growth in faith and discipleship, on the other hand, can be accommodated through a series of covenant or Bible study groups that meet at times other than the regular youth meeting time. These youth can then become models for the rest of the group in terms of what faith growth means to them.

60

46 How do we strike a good balance between spiritual growth, learning, and fun?

First, you have to determine what a good balance is and why you want it. The why part is the easiest. A good balance helps youth mature in faith. It is a bit harder to determine what a good balance is. In part, that depends on the age of your group, where they are in faith maturity, and where you feel comfortable leading them. But let's say a good balance would be 33%–33%–34%. How do you strike that balance?

Remember, in a good game plan (or master plan; see Questions 28 and 92), you know that you do not have to do everything in every part of your youth ministry. For example, the heavy emphasis on learning is in what happens on Sunday morning, so you do not have to focus as heavily on learning in your fellowship times. However, you will want to include at least some learning time for youth who come only to fellowship groups.

My personal bias would be to have the fun time segue into learning, perhaps a community-building game that includes both reflection on the game and reflection on how the game relates to Christian faith. I would have a specific time for worship and prayer, with youth assuming as much leadership as they are ready to take. But I would also allow for spontaneous moments when it seems appropriate to stop whatever you are doing and give thanks to God.

47 How do we inspire youth to want to learn about God when they have "more interesting" things on their minds?

You do not have the skills and equipment to compete with most of those things. For example, you cannot compete with the entertainment world. And most youth have personal computers that allow them to do things, both serious and fun, far beyond what the church can offer. One of the things youth think about most is the opposite sex.

One way to deal with the problem of "more interesting" things is to remind yourselves that there are some things only the church can do. One of these is worship. A nearby youth group sets aside the third Sunday of every month as worship night. Youth are in charge of planning and leading the service. Each youth is invited to light a votive candle, put it on the altar as a way of saying "I'm here, God," and then to spend some time in prayer. That night has the best attendance of the month. And the youth who are there only for fun get involved in this worship time.

61

Out of that kind of experience comes questions that youth raise about God and life. So, some months, that youth group sets aside the fourth Sunday as question time. More than one cut-up has found her or himself asking heavy questions about God in this period.

48 **How do we help youth grow spiritually when so many other activities take up their time?**

One of the most important issues with which they deal is the use of time. Youth cannot do everything; they have to make choices. One way we can help them grow spiritually in the light of time pressures is to help them develop good decision-making skills. Another is to help them learn how to set priorities: What is the most important thing for me long-term? What is the most important thing for me this Wednesday night? If youth say something else is more important this Sunday, we have to accept that choice.

49 **How do we have an effective devotional time without losing their interest?**

At least two different approaches should be considered here. One of them is ritual, since youth are fascinated by mystery and ritual. The candle-lighting ceremony in Question 47 is a good example. Also effective is the full ritual for Holy Communion (not the shortcut version that many pastors are now using in worship).

A second approach is to invite youth to take leadership in planning and conducting worship. If they have prepared the talk for a previous week, they will listen carefully this week because they know how much effort a friend has put into planning this talk. They want to be respectful of her time and want others to be respectful of their time. This is not just a gimmick to hold interest for the devotional time; it is an important way to help youth grow in faith.

50 **How do we teach prayer to this age group?**

Teach prayer by praying in a variety of ways, in order to engage youth. A good way to begin is by having a circle prayer, with each person saying thank you for something or someone. Circle prayers can be expanded to include joys and concerns as well.

As part of worship time, ask for prayer concerns and joys. Many of these will seem trivial compared with the needs of the world, but they are important to youth. Pray for each of these by name. Yes, this means you will have to take notes while youth are naming concerns. Or, as each concern is named, the entire group can say, in unison, "Hear our prayer, O Lord," or something similar. Obviously, a prayer naming the concerns will teach youth more about praying, but anything that involves them in prayer is important.

Allow time for silent prayer and/or guided prayers or meditations. Play background music (such as Gregorian chants), put the room in semi-darkness, and use a lot of candles. Youth love ritual and mystery that is typified by music and candles. They can also be encouraged to pray silently during periods of quiet. At first, make these quiet times short, such as two minutes or fewer. After youth become comfortable with quiet, you can stretch out the time (with some groups, even as long as thirty minutes on occasion).

Finally, ask youth to pray aloud. Their prayers will not be polished; in fact, they may be full of "like, you know" and "uh," but that is all right. The key is that they are praying. Encourage every effort at prayer.

Questions You Didn't Ask

51

What is all this about faith maturity? Should we be concerned about it? How do we make it happen?

At the most basic level, faith maturity is a way of describing what happens when we try to live out the great commandments: to love God with all our heart and mind and soul and strength, and our neighbor as ourselves (Mark 12:28-31). Jesus' summary of the Torah and the Prophets reminds us that, in faith, there is a vertical dimension of relationship with God and a horizontal dimension of relationship with other people (and with the natural order, the environment). So, yes, this is something about which you should be concerned in your ministry. How does it work?

Faith maturity is also about goals, visions, and dreams for ministry. All of us want numbers because numbers represent people, and we want to reach as many people as possible. But we also want to help them grow in faith and discipleship. So, how do we do that?

John Wesley, the founder of what became The United Methodist Church, said that moving toward maturity means engaging in works of piety and works of mercy. By works of piety, he meant

63

- prayer, both private and public;
- Bible study;
- regular worship with the congregation;
- regular participation in the Lord's Supper;
- Christian conversation, by which he meant being involved in a small group where people both support one another in their faith struggles and hold one another accountable when they are less than faithful.

By works of mercy, Wesley meant such things as feeding the hungry, clothing the naked, caring for the sick and those in prison, and generally doing good to all those around us. He considered those works to be something that his followers did on a regular, ongoing basis, not just once in a while. In our day, that includes working in soup kitchens, being on mission work teams, repairing homes in the community, working on Habitat for Humanity houses, or volunteering at the local homeless shelter or the community hospital.

Today, we might want to add a third dimension: works of justice. These are the actions in which we engage that seek to change the social, political, and economic systems that cause people to be hungry, cold, naked, homeless, sick. A part of works of justice involves teaching youth about biblical concepts of justice and how they apply to real life. Another part could involve writing letters about an impending political decision that affects the lives of people in your area. A third might be working to establish a youth activity center that would attract high-risk youth and offer them an alternative to destructive behaviors.

What Makes a Good Counselor?

This question is about good counselors, suggesting adults who work with fellowship groups. But almost everything we say about counselors also applies to adults who teach youth Sunday school, teach confirmation classes, or work with youth in other ways.

52 What are the most important attributes of a good counselor?

People will always answer that question in a variety ways, and you may think of other attributes that are important for you. Even given all the potential differences, there is a kind of unspoken consensus on key attributes. Here are the top five.

Good counselors

- Are comfortable being adults. That sounds obvious, but adult workers with youth who are trying to relive their own adolescence can destroy a youth group without even trying. So, good counselors do not have to be youth; they do not even have to be young. They especially do not have to act like youth. They need to be comfortable being who they are, which is adults.
- Love youth. A half-dozen informal polls among youth show that the attribute they most want in adults is love of youth. This ranked far

65

above biblical knowledge, awareness of the latest music, the ability to stay up all night, and everything else on the list. Love in this context means caring about who they are, being willing to confront them when they are out of line, holding them up when they are falling apart, and being there for them all the time.

- Have a growing faith in God through Jesus Christ. That does not mean they have to have a perfect faith or know all the answers. Nor does it mean they have to be evangelizing or witnessing all the time. It does mean they know Jesus Christ as Savior and Lord and are growing in their understanding and practice of their faith. Good counselors can be beginners in the faith, if they are open to growing.

- Are willing to commit time and energy to youth ministry. How often have you heard an adult say, "I want materials that don't take any time to prepare"? Friends, to care is to prepare. When we show up unprepared for a youth meeting, we have already told youth we do not care about them, or about their growth in faith. It takes time and energy to be a good counselor, not just for meetings and car washes but for preparing diligently for what is going to happen when the group comes together.

- Are flexible and have tolerance for ambiguity. Flexibility means being able to shift gears in the middle of a discussion, if necessary. Youth often ask questions that are unrelated to the topic at hand but that are important to them. Good counselors are willing to put aside their careful preparation and deal with the question. When I was teaching senior highs, our number-one rule was, You can ask any question you want, about any topic you want, at any time you want. We did not always deal with the question when it was asked, but we always dealt with it. A tolerance for ambiguity means that we are willing to not always have all the answers. Good counselors and teachers do not have an agenda; that is, they do not have set answers they want youth to be able to absorb and repeat back. Rather, they recognize that there are a lot of gray areas in life and are comfortable with that kind of ambiguity.

How do I stay in touch with the problems youth are having?

53 This question really has two parts. The first part of the question is, How do I stay in touch with the problems youth (as a classification of people) are having? To do that, read newspapers, news magazines, magazines that specialize in youth. Surf the

66

Web for articles about youth and the problems they face. If you search diligently, you will probably be overwhelmed by the amount of material you find. (See the list of resources and websites on youth and youth ministry, on pages 119–25.)

The second part of the question is, How do I stay in touch with the problems faced by the youth with whom I work? Be present to youth and willing to listen to them. Work on establishing relationships of trust and understanding. Spend some time on youth turf: ball games, concerts, plays, and other school events. You probably will not spend a lot of time talking to youth at these events, but they will know you are present, which translates into caring about them. Know where they have jobs, and drop in to buy a frozen custard or a pair of shoelaces from them or to say, "Hi. How's it going?"

When you establish an awareness of youth activities and a presence among youth, you will find that the doors to staying in touch swing wide open. Youth will tell you about their problems, and you will probably learn more than you thought you wanted to know.

In addition, concerned questions help you stay in touch. "How's it going?" is sometimes all the question you need to invite youth to open up. When you begin to know youth better, you can quietly ask individuals specific questions: How did the audition work out? Are you still struggling with your attitude toward your science teacher? How is it with you and your Mom?

General questions as a part of community building or devotional time at meetings can also elicit awareness of youth problems. One youth leader begins every meeting by asking, "How was the week? What went well? What was a bummer?" He often goes on to ask, "Where did you see God at work this week? What was God saying to you in the activities of the week?"

How do I keep from being intimidated by youth?

54

Good question. Let's start with you. What is there about youth that you find intimidating? Is it that they have so much energy? or that they seem so different? or that you are afraid they will not like you? One factor in intimidation may be not knowing what you will find to talk about.

That last statement also gives us a major clue in how to avoid intimidation. Ask youth about themselves. Try to find out what they are doing, what they like, what is going on in their lives. Ask open-ended questions,

67

or at least questions that require more than a yes or no answer. Begin with simple stuff: What year in school are you? What are your favorite subjects? What extra-curricular activities are you involved in? What do you like to do when you do not have to do anything?

You will find that not only are you not intimidated by youth but that you are making friends and building relationships that will last for a long time and enrich your ministry with youth. Remember, youth want you to like them as much as you want them to like you (well, almost as much). Having said that, here is a hard statement: Youth do not have to like you; and if being liked is your goal, you may discover that you are always intimidated. The goal should be that youth respect you as a person, as a leader, as someone who is struggling and growing in faith, just as they are. If they also like you, that is a bonus.

But there is still that other intimidation factor: What happens when we stand up in front of that group of twenty (or sixty, or one hundred) youth on Sunday night (or Sunday morning, or whenever) and try to hold their attention for whatever is supposed to happen? That can be really intimidating, particularly when there are about as many conversations going on as there are youth in the group. What helps here? One thing to do is be prepared. If you know what you are going to do and why you are going to do it, that will go a long way toward dealing with the intimidation factor. Another thing that helps is the relationships you are building with individual youth. You know there are people in the group who respect you and will give you a chance to do your thing.

You should also have a nonthreatening way to quiet the conversations and focus attention on worship, Bible study, announcements, or whatever is coming next (see Question 19).

Above all, remember that you are a person with gifts and graces for ministry. When you feel overwhelmed or intimidated, keep in mind that God called you to this ministry. (And you thought it was the youth director twisting your arm, right?)

55 How do I get on the youth level to improve communication?

There is good news and bad news here. Let's start with the bad news. There is no magic youth level that, if you get there, will make communication easy. You are not a teen, and trying to talk like one will not help. Remember, one of the marks of a good counselor is that you are comfortable being an adult (see Question 52). And good communication does not necessarily come from using the right slang. If you feel uncomfortable using certain words and phrases because they are just not you, do not use them. Being uncomfortable will hinder communication.

So, what is the good news? If you are open and willing to listen, you will find communication is pretty easy (see Question 54). Find out what your youth are interested in. Talk to them outside youth meetings: after worship, in the halls at church, on the street, at their work, wherever you meet them. Ask them about their world, and see if they will invite you in. One Sunday school teacher, in an attempt to increase interest and improve communication, invited youth to bring CDs of songs they really liked. They each played a song for the group, talked about what the song said, explained why they liked it, and told if the song reminded them of anything they had heard about in the Bible or Christian faith. Communication was much freer after about six weeks of talking about music. You could also talk about current movies. Even if you have not seen the movies, you can ask intelligent questions about what they like about a movie or what the movie said to them.

Be honest with youth about what you do and do not know. They are the world's greatest experts at spotting phonies. However, you should have limits on your honesty (see Question 58).

Give youth some space. Do not push too hard for communication. Lay out some openers. If nothing happens, be patient. Listen when they do talk to you.

And here is the really good news: Youth do want to talk to adults they trust. If you can establish the foundation for a good relationship, they will seek you out to talk.

How do I avoid getting discouraged?

56 This is the greatest occupational hazard for youth workers, both professionals and volunteers. You put so much into what you are doing and see so little in the way of results. One of the great drawbacks of working with youth is that someone else sees the results. Although you work with youth for years, they often do not discover how important all the things you tried to teach them are until they graduate from high school and leave home. When they are successful in overcoming temptation and struggling with life questions, they rarely come back and say thank you. I once sent e-mail devotionals to college students from my group every week for five years. After about three years, one youth wrote back to say how much the devotionals had meant in his life and how much they had helped him in his struggles to hold onto his faith in a university setting. But only that one youth ever said thanks. However, several others wrote back, and we had discussions by e-mail about problems they were facing. This is another way of knowing that you did something right. Something like that goes a long way toward overcoming discouragement.

Probably the biggest discouragement is when youth go to a rally or an evangelistic event led by a parachurch group and come back converted. They are full of praise for the speaker who led them to Christ, and you are burning up because someone else gets the credit for what you had been trying to do for years. My friend, you probably deserve most of the credit, although you may never get it. All the loving work you did with that youth over the years prepared the way for the breakthrough at that event. As Paul said to the Corinthians, "I planted, Apollos watered, but God gave the growth" (1 Corinthians 3:6). If we can give God the praise, instead of being burned up about a situation like this, we will be taking much better care of ourselves.

Then there is the week-to-week discouragement of working hard to prepare a good Sunday school lesson, a good program, a good Bible study that youth do not come to or pay attention to, and you go home wondering why you even bother. That is the kind of discouragement that strikes deep into our hearts and burns us out. How do you deal with that? Here are several suggestions:

- Stay in touch with your own spiritual life. Give the situation to God. Gain strength through prayer. Give yourself permission to take time away for personal retreats, in order to build your faith relationship.
- Develop a peer support group. Meet regularly (once a month) with the other youth leaders for prayer, planning, and mutual support. Listen to one another's hurts and disappointments. (This is not a gripe session, however. Be sure you offer understanding and help to one another, instead of trying to top one another's stories of how bad things are.) What if you are the only person in your church who works with youth? Meet with youth workers in other churches. Go to lunch, or whatever, on a regular basis. Pray together, tell one another stories, lean on one another. Knowing you are not alone and that you have friends who understand goes a long way toward dealing with burnout.
- Take advantage of district and conference opportunities for youth workers. Meeting with people from a wider area provides another level

70

of support. You will get good ideas for programs and for how to deal with problems from a wider circle of peers. Some district/conference groups plan a two- or three-day retreat for youth workers each year, just to get away to play and pray.
- Find a mentor in your congregation to whom you can pour out your hurts and dreams. Sometimes an older person no longer has the energy to work with large groups of youth directly but can be a source of support and wisdom for those who do. Identify a person in your congregation whom you trust to listen to you and help you walk through your struggles. Ask this person if you can meet with him or her monthly to talk and pray about your situation.
- Participate regularly in an exercise program. Regular exercise, whether on your own or as part of a group, not only helps your physical health but also gives you energy to deal with emotional and relationship issues. Walking, riding a bike, working out at the gym, swimming, or whatever you like to do—stay with it for both physical and emotional health.

What about long-term burnout?

57 Years of working with youth workers across the denomination suggests that the key to avoiding burnout is to plan for a long ministry in the same place. This means that you do not have to worry too much about the Roman candle syndrome, which begins with a lot of energy and enthusiasm but then does not go beyond enthusiasm. Youth workers who do this attract a lot of youth and develop a lot of energy in the group, but they also burn out about as quickly as a Roman candle. So, what do you do?

- Follow all the suggestions in Question 56 about caring for your health, having a peer support group and a mentor, and staying in touch with your personal spiritual life.
- Plan long-range (see Questions 25–31 and 92). If you know where you are going so that you do not have to start from scratch every week, you are already ahead of the burnout problem. Frantic scrambling week after week will burn out the most dedicated youth leader. When you finish a session with youth, knowing what you will be doing in the next session (at least in broad outline) takes away a lot of pressure and stress. A long-range plan reminds you that the measure of what you do is not what happened or did not happen last week. If your measure of success is how well one lesson or program went, you will find yourself on a continual roller coaster, going from highs to lows and back again.

If you can see that you are making progress, however slow, toward a long-range goal, you will not feel as emotionally exhausted by the highs and lows.

- Work your plan and do not deviate from it for everything that comes along. However, there are always exceptions. A tragic death of a high school student, an international disaster, or a crisis in the church will mean you drop whatever you had planned for that Sunday morning (or evening) and deal with the immediate crisis. Then go back to your plan the next week. Exceptions should be exceptional and not knee-jerk responses to whatever comes along during the week. Youth are not always as traumatized by national and international events as we think they will be.

- Remember your own spiritual growth and nurture. Your own faith maturity is important not only to youth but also to you. Learning to depend on God for strength, for results, and for the long-term maturity of your youth sets you free from having to make everything happen.

58 How do we answer questions youth ask about our pasts, when we made the same, or worse, mistakes as the ones we see them making? How can we help them really know us without making ourselves seem like bad models?

Ask yourself, *How does it help my ministry if youth know I once smoked pot or danced half-naked in the rain at Woodstock?* We are often tempted to tell youth all the bad mistakes in judgment we made so that they will know we are real people. Or, worse, we tell them, in detail, all about our sins so that they will appreciate more the story of our conversion/salvation. The danger is that when we lay out our past, they do not hear the real message we are trying to communicate. If you talk about smoking pot, drinking, and so forth, they are likely to pass on the message that you talked about pot and stuff like that and never communicate how God helped you change your life. Or, some youth may even lose respect for you and stop listening to anything you say. (They do have high standards to which they hold adults.) If being a model is the issue, focus on the positive. Tell them about how God worked, and works, in your life to help you grow in faith, to help you avoid temptation, to help you make a fresh start when you made mistakes. Use the great hymn "Amazing Grace" as your model. The hymn's writer spends the first part of the hymn talking about his sin, and the rest praising God. "I once was

72

lost" is an admission that sin had been active in his life, without going into a lot of explicit details. That should be a model for us as well.

59 How do I keep youth active when I am burned out and do not feel like being active myself?

The obvious response is a question: Why not take some time off? If you are burned out and do not feel like being active, that is going to be clear to the youth with whom you work. We all need a break from time to time. Why not sabbaticals for youth leaders?

But what do you do if you are one of only two leaders for your group and there are no other volunteers in the congregation who would fill in while you take a sabbatical? The first thing you need to do is decide why you feel burned out: Is the burnout because you are just plain tired? Is it because you are out of ideas for youth lessons/programs? Or is it because you feel as if you are banging your head against a wall with the youth, and you are ready for some major pain relief?

If you are tired, either physically or emotionally, talk about it with the youth. They know there is something wrong already, so level with them and ask them for help. Maybe they can take on some of the responsibilities of setting up the room or handling the ushering at worship without your standing over them. This could be an opportunity for youth to develop leadership skills and give you a rest at the same time. And, if they become more active in the process, you have won on three fronts: You get a little rest, they take on some leadership responsibility, and they become more active.

If you are out of ideas for lessons/programs, there are a couple things you might try. One would be to say to your youth, "Hey, I'm fresh out of ideas for programs/lessons. What are some topics you would really like to talk about?" A second possibility would be to check out websites to see what kinds of program resources are out there, and what topics appeal to you. (One website that can give you a lot of ideas and resources is www.ileadyouth.com.) One reason we burn out is that we keep trying to reinvent the wheel all the time.

If you feel as if you are banging your head against a wall, and you just do not want to fight that anymore, take some time off. Or, be honest with the youth and tell them how you feel and why you feel that way. Tell them you do not want to be tired and grouchy, and you sure do not want to let them down. But you feel as if they let you down when they do not cooperate or when they do not talk without prodding from you (or whatever

73

your specific hurt is). Do not try to make them feel guilty so that they will straighten up. Just tell them how you feel about what is going on, and ask for their help in thinking of ways to deal with the situation. Skip the conversation about whose fault it is and go straight to problem solving.

60 How do we help volunteers come out of their safety zones and try new things?

We would all love to know the answer to that one. Adults do have comfort/safety zones, and it is hard for us to even admit that, let alone take the risk to try something new. One way to go at it takes a lot of time and energy, but it works well:
- I will do it; you watch me.
- I will do it; you help me.
- You do it; I will help you.
- You do it; I will do something else.

That takes a lot of time, particularly if you multiply by several volunteers and have to go through the process every time a new experience comes along. You may want to hold it in reserve for major issues, such as retreat planning, but it does leave better-trained volunteers in your wake.

61 How do we help volunteers be less judgmental? They feel overwhelmed and respond by being critical.

One volunteer is critical about the way girls dress. She almost never says anything to the girls, usually only to other adult leaders. But she is concerned about the kind of behavior she is afraid might result from the way girls dress. She is correct in thinking that girls sometimes wear clothes that are far too revealing, in a situation where hormones are already raging in youth. (Dress that seems inappropriate in boys is so for reasons different from being too revealing.) In fact, this volunteer is worried about how her teenage son, who is part of the group, will respond to the way girls dress.

Another volunteer is ultraconscious of the way youth behave. Most youth, particularly junior highs, can do several things at once and not miss a word the leader is saying while they are seemingly not paying attention. Some adults are all right with this and just keep on, knowing that youth are listening in spite of appearances. When volunteers do not see that youth can do several things at once, they may become critical of both the youth and other adults who do not seem to want youth to behave.

74

Almost all volunteers who are judgmental/critical about youth are so because they care and worry about the consequences of what seems to them inappropriate behavior. So, a part of the reality behind this question is a lack of consensus on what is appropriate. What do we do about that?

One simple solution is to have regular meetings of all people involved with youth so that anyone with concerns can air them with the group. A discussion among adults about what is appropriate and not appropriate, with reasons people feel the way they do, should help clear the air and relieve some concerns. But that, in itself, is not enough. Go beyond the airing of concerns to build understanding about youth behavior, how youth develop and learn, and, if necessary, some kind of consensus on what adults will agree is inappropriate behavior. You certainly do not want to get in a situation where you have strict dress codes for youth group. A quiet discussion with some girls who are leaders in the group might help the immediate situation. If adult leaders can agree on what behaviors are inappropriate during times of discussion or worship, they could communicate their agreement to the youth so that everyone knows what behavior will be called to account. It gets trickier if one adult is more comfortable with relaxed behavior than other adults are (see Questions 12–19, on dealing with discipline).

A major issue for many volunteers is how to deal with PDAs (public displays of affection). Nagging youth about inappropriate behavior is not a good way to deal with this issue. Many youth leaders deal with this by establishing the no-purpling rule. Boys are blue and girls are pink, and you get purple when you combine the two. This is a fun way to set up a rule that is easy to understand. Youth themselves are more than willing to help enforce a rule like this. You can also use it for establishing limits on who is in what hall during retreats or camps. A rule that youth can enforce themselves takes a lot of pressure off the volunteer leaders and their concerns about appropriate behavior.

62 How can fellowship leaders know what is happening in Sunday school (so that we do not duplicate)?

A good way to do this is to have regular meetings of all adults who work with youth. Part of the agenda should be planning for the next month so that everyone knows what everyone else is doing (see Questions 28 and 30). One of the benefits of working as a team and having regular meetings is that you have some assurance you are not in it alone. You do

75

not have to do everything in fellowship groups, because a part of the essential learning in faith is happening in Sunday school, in confirmation, in choir, and so forth. When you know what the other groups are doing, you are more secure and relaxed about the part of the load you carry.

63 How do we know when to tell a parent something that a youth has confided in us?

Here is what sounds like a flip answer, but it is deadly serious: whenever you are ready to stop working with youth. Nothing destroys trust in a leader quicker than breaking confidences. It will end any effective ministry you could have with that youth and probably with the entire group. Never tell a parent something a youth has told you in confidence. If you think the parents need to know, talk with the youth about the need to tell her or his parents. Assure her or him that you will go along for the conversation and offer support. In situations such as pregnancy, for example, it is vital that the parents know; but the teen should be the one to tell the parents. You can be available for support, but do not be the one to tell the parents.

Now, having said that, there are two exceptions. The first is if you feel the youth is in danger of doing her or himself serious harm (suicide or attempted suicide). The second is if there is clear evidence that the youth is using/abusing drugs, which can also be deadly. In these cases, you have a moral obligation to tell parents, because of your concern for the life of the youth.

One more exception exists that does not involve telling the parents. That exception is if you suspect, or know, that a youth is being abused physically or sexually by a family member. In that case, you need to involve the local police or social service agencies. Your pastor will know which is the appropriate agency to call in your community. This is a matter not only of protection for the youth but also a situation in which (depending on your state) you may be legally bound to report suspected abuse.

Recruiting and Training Volunteers

How do we recruit volunteers?

64 First, let's talk about how *not* to recruit volunteers. Do not go begging: "We need someone to teach junior highs, and I've tried everyone I can think of. Won't you please help us out?" The natural, and correct, response to that kind of approach is, "Sorry. If I'm the bottom of the barrel, you don't want me, anyway. I think I'll just stay with my adult class." And do not make an announcement in worship: "Fall Sunday school starts next week, and we still need a teacher for the senior highs. If you'd be willing to help, please see me after worship." That is a bad approach for at least two reasons. First, it carries a message to the senior highs that they are not important and that anyone can teach them. Second, you have to take whoever volunteers, and the people who volunteer will inevitably be the last people in the world you would want to have teaching your senior highs. Do not focus only on young adults. Some of them will make excellent youth leaders, but some of them will be people who want to relive their own youth, to be one of the youth. (See Question 52 for more about attributes of a good adult leader.) Do not tell them that working with youth is easy and will not take any time to prepare. Remember, to care means to prepare. Be honest about what you are asking volunteers to do and how much time and energy you are expecting them to contribute.

So, how do you recruit volunteers? It is an ongoing process, but let's take a one-year approach. Start early. If you need new teachers for September, start recruiting in February or March. Begin with prayer, asking for God's guidance as you seek to engage people in ministry with youth. Then make a list of the people you believe would be the best possible prospects for teaching (see Questions 52–63). Go to each of these people and talk about what you want him or her to do and why. One approach I have found successful is to say, "What I'm about to ask may be the most important thing God is calling you to do in the next year." This identifies the recruitment process as part of living out our discipleship in response to God's call. Lay out the big picture, telling what your plan is for Christian education with youth. Give the person a copy of the plan to study. Show the person where you think he or she would best fit in with the plan. Be specific about what you would expect in terms of time, energy, and enthusiasm. Be clear that resources are available. I once recruited a teacher and found out two weeks later that she thought she was going to have to write her own resources. Be clear that you expect him or her to use the resources the church provides and not to just go off on his or her own whenever an idea strikes. Talk to volunteers about the training opportunities that are available for them (this may mean you'll have to create some training sessions) and what kind of ongoing support is available.

Remember that many adults are reluctant to commit to working with youth because they are not sure of their own skills and knowledge. Do not tell them this does not matter, for they know it does. Talk to prospective adult leaders about the gifts and graces you see that they have for working with youth. You may know that they have a gift for teaching. Or, they may have the kind of personality that you know will resonate with youth. They may have important knowledge in areas that are crucial to your game plan for the next couple years. (Graduates of DISCIPLE Bible study, for example, probably know more about the Bible than do most other adults in the church.) Assure prospective leaders that there are specific opportunities for them to learn those skills/knowledge about which they are concerned. Be sure you can follow up on that assurance with specific training events.

All that takes time and energy on your part, time you might think you could better spend actually doing ministry with youth. Recruiting and training strong lay leadership *is* doing ministry.

What are some different ways to recruit and train volunteers?

65

Let's assume that this question is different from the previous one and means something like, "Are there some new and/or unusual ways of recruiting and training volunteers?" We will divide the answer into two parts: one dealing with recruitment, the other with training.

1. What if, as a key element in your recruiting program, you noticed which adults in the congregation make a point of talking to youth? Those people would be prime candidates to recruit for youth leaders/ Sunday school teachers. You may even want to ask the youth who they would suggest as potential youth leaders. Another possibility is to recruit parents. Several youth ministers with large confirmation classes use the parents of the confirmands as small-group leaders, support people, presenters, and so forth. Many of those parents then volunteer to stay with the youth in that class as teachers through their junior and senior high school years. The models we have seen are in large churches, but the basic idea could work in almost any size church.

2. Another possibility is to encourage your congregation to develop a series of courses on spiritual gifts, in which each participant takes a spiritual gifts inventory and the results are entered into the church's database. Check out which people show teaching as a spiritual gift. (In fact, this could be a gift you could give to the congregation: Advocate that every person in the congregation, over the next three years, take a spiritual gifts inventory and be involved in a small-group discussion about what their gifts mean. This could be a great resource for the entire church.) Use training as a recruiting tool. Invite people you think would be good youth leaders to take part in a workshop for training leaders. Many people say no to being a youth leader because they do not know what to do or how to work with youth. Once they have the opportunity to explore some basic skills, they may be more open to stepping up as leaders themselves. And do not forget older adults. Many of us think we have to have younger adults, who will identify with the youth. You definitely need some younger adults, who have more energy; but you also need some older adults with more experience and wisdom as a balance. Someone who is sixty may not want to hang out all night at a lock-in, but he or she can offer a great deal of experience in other settings. An old joke says that the

79

best leaders for junior highs are people their grandparents' age, because they have a common enemy. Actually, studies in generational theory have shown there is a solid sociological basis for that old joke (see Question 96), so take advantage of it.

Now, what about training? First, you need to have all your youth leaders—old and new—involved in Safe Sanctuaries training (see Question 97). Safe Sanctuaries policies and procedures are about protecting both youth and adults from abuse and/or accusations of abuse. Your annual conference may have people or resources that can help you develop policies for your church. More and more churches are requiring all adults who work with children and youth to have this kind of training before they can serve in any volunteer or paid position with children and youth.

Second, you need training in skills for working with youth. Adults want to know how to talk with youth, how to deal with discipline problems, how to get skills in teaching and leading, and so forth.

Third, you need training in content. Many adults are reluctant to work with youth because they do not know enough about the Bible themselves. Provide regular opportunities for adult workers to study specific content. One way to do this might be to have monthly or quarterly training sessions that would focus on the specific content to be taught the next month or quarter. This would allow adults to explore the biblical and theological content of upcoming sessions and gain some confidence in their ability to teach that content to youth. (See Question 69 for more detailed models.)

66. How do we find and train leaders youth will accept?

This calls for a counter-question: What are the dynamics behind wanting leaders youth will accept? Does it mean youth will accept only certain personality types? or age levels? or levels of skill? Do youth have hidden criteria that determines whether or not adults will be accepted? Questions such as those will lead you down a dangerous path, where you allow youth's acceptance (real or imagined) to dictate who you ask to serve as leaders. That does not mean youth should not have some voice in decisions about their leaders, but they should never have veto power.

Here is the good news: The quality youth want most in adults who work with them is love for youth. If they are loved, they will accept a lot of inadequate training and knowledge. As a youth, I had a youth

80

fellowship leader who had none of the skills and gifts that we often look for today. She did not have a lot of charisma, did not have great speaking skills, did not have a deep fund of knowledge about the faith (although she knew more than we thought she did at the time). What she did have was a depth of love for us and faith in us that helped us be better than we were. She supported us as we searched for answers to questions. She made sure we had logistical support to attend district and conference youth events and to get to camp in the summer. She helped us raise funds for mission projects, and she taught us to pray. By almost any criteria of initial youth acceptance, she would not be on most of our rosters of youth leaders. Yet, she was one of the most effective youth leaders I have ever known.

So, what kind of teacher/counselor will youth accept? As we said in Question 52, you need to consider some characteristics of good counselors/teachers as you recruit leaders. Because those characteristics are so important, they are repeated here.

Good counselors
- Are comfortable being adults.
- Love youth.
- Have a growing faith in God through Jesus Christ.
- Are willing to commit time and energy to youth ministry.
- Are flexible and have tolerance for ambiguity.

67 How do we keep leaders? After a year, they say, "I've had my turn."

Part of the answer is the distinction between recruiting leaders and filling slots. If you simply fill slots so that an adult is in every position, you will probably have to fill most of those slots again next year. If you recruit leaders who love youth and are willing to make commitments to care and to prepare (see Question 86), you will have a better retention rate. Both take time. One approach takes time every year; the other takes more time in the beginning but less time in the second and third years.

Obviously, job transfers, increased job responsibilities, and other factors outside your control are going to affect your retention rate. I try to keep a pool of leaders who have had Safe Sanctuaries training and some training in basic skills so that I have trained people to fall back on if a leader is suddenly transferred. It might also be useful to have twice as many trained leaders as you need so that they can rotate out every couple years. Most adults, even those who love working with youth, also need time to learn with other adults. This is particularly true for youth Sunday school teachers. If you can tell them they have a year's sabbatical after every two years they teach, they may be more willing to make longer-term commitments.

Honest appreciation is also a simple way to keep leaders. One congregation that was faced with the problem of finding new teachers for youth Sunday school every year solved the problem by having a teacher appreciation banquet every year. Youth and their parents hosted the dinner (a potluck so that no one was stuck in the kitchen cleaning up) and invited the teachers and their families as special guests. Teachers were given corsages or boutonnieres and were seated at a head table, while youth were assigned to keep water glasses and coffee cups filled. The pastor and Christian education director gave speeches of appreciation, naming specific contributions each teacher had made. Youth also gave public thanks for what the teachers had done. Finally, each teacher was given a plaque engraved with his or her name and a special thanks for being a teacher. That church had an amazing rate of retention. Another congregation gave each adult worker with youth a canvas tote bag for carrying supplies. The bag said "You're Special—You Help Our Youth." This helped the congregation become more aware of who was working with youth so that they could thank the volunteers.

68 How do we get volunteers to make serious commitments long-term?

A key part of that commitment is recruiting the right people in the first place (see Questions 65 and 66). Another part is being sure volunteers get the support they need. Support includes training, resources, a sense of knowing where they fit into the big picture of Christian education with youth, and appreciation for their efforts. When you recruit, ask them for a minimum of two years' service.

69 What about models for training? What should volunteers know?

Taking the second part of the question first, volunteers should know

- Safe Sanctuaries policies and procedures;
- Basic communication skills with youth;
- A variety of teaching methods;

82

- Something about the ways youth learn;
- How what they are doing fits into the big picture of Christian education with youth;
- Basic knowledge of biblical and theological concepts;
- How to find the answers to questions youth ask.

How do you train busy people in all those skills and areas of knowledge? They will give up before they ever get started. Well, sure, they will give up if the approach is as blunt as what is listed above. However, you are more subtle than that, so you will not tell them all that before you start. Simply assure volunteers that they will get training in what they need to know and will have support in future crises. Consider the following models as possibilities for your program.

1. Safe Sanctuaries Policies and Procedures

Safe Sanctuaries policies and procedures are about protecting youth so that the church, either on-site or off-site, is a safe place for them to be. It is also about protecting adults who work with youth. Recent public revelations about sexual abuse in both Protestant and Catholic churches remind us that we all need to be more vigilant about protecting our youth—and ourselves. Creating Safe Sanctuaries involves both policy and procedure for ministries with children and youth. Policy is the structure in which the issues are spelled out. It answers the questions about who, what, and why. Procedures spell out how your church implements the policy. It answers the questions about when, where, and how. Workers with youth should be trained in both policies and procedures. Many annual conferences have training materials that you can use in your local church. These materials include information on state laws, how to be aware of signs of abuse, and sometimes even first aid.

2. An Introductory Retreat

Schedule a weekend retreat late in the summer every year for your teachers and fellowship group leaders, both veterans and rookies. If possible, plan the retreat for a Friday overnight and all day Saturday, at a site away from the church and distractions. Arrange for childcare where it is needed. Recruit a team of youth parents or other adults to take care of meals, snacks, and other logistical issues so that the teachers can focus full time on learning. Set aside Friday evening for building community and laying the foundations for the retreat. This time could include inviting teachers and leaders to raise issues and questions that concern them. If their issues will be dealt with during the retreat, tell them to expect that. If not, tell them they will be dealt with during the coming year. Also on Friday night, lay out the big picture of Christian education with youth in your church. This could include distributing copies of your master plan.

On Saturday, have a series of ninety-minute sessions that include Bible study, introduction to the resources for the next quarter and how to use them, teaching/learning methods, support systems in your church, and other topics that fit your situation. Include time for rest and reflection as well as for work.

3. Monthly or Quarterly Updates

In this model, you can do two things. First, teaching teams can take some time to go over the material they will be teaching in the next month or quarter, noting what biblical and theological background material they might still need, what teaching methods they are not familiar with and could use a little coaching on, and so forth. (Actually, it would be ideal to do this every month, but time pressures probably will dictate quarterly meetings.) Second, plan to spend some time, as a part of each meeting, giving your leaders some training on such topics as multiple intelligences, the Millennial Generation, a new teaching skill, or other area of concern. Include a time for dealing with specific questions and concerns raised by the teachers and leaders themselves.

4. Bible Study

Many teachers still feel inadequate when it comes to teaching the Bible to youth. (This will be true even of DISCIPLE Bible study graduates.) From time to time, invite youth teachers and leaders to a special Bible study session. This is not an ongoing weekly study, although it could be if the teachers request it. Rather, it is an occasional study that has the following characteristics:

- It involves an extended period of time (two or more hours).
- It focuses on a biblical theme, such as covenant, grace, or salvation.
- It has some depth of study and learning.
- It may involve the pastor or other skilled Bible teacher from the congregation.
- It may or may not be related to biblical themes coming up in youth studies.
- It is not a how-to session but one designed to enrich the teacher's own faith.

84

Involving Parents in Youth Ministry

Why do we want to get parents more involved?

70 First, are the parents churched or unchurched? The answer to that question will determine, to a large degree, why you want to get them involved in youth ministry.

If the parents are unchurched, getting them involved with youth ministry may be a step toward getting them involved in the church. With unchurched parents, you want to move gradually and ask them to help in nonthreatening ways. For example, invite them to youth softball games or other sports activities. Ask them to help drive youth to skating rinks, concerts, and so forth and to help provide snacks or meals for youth meetings. As they become involved in youth activities, other parents will invite them to worship and Sunday school. Because they already know people in the church, they will not feel as unsure about attending worship. Involving them in youth ministry can move them into personal involvement with the church.

If the parents are already churched, you want to involve them in youth ministry so that they can live out their own commitments to their youth. In the service of the Baptismal Covenant, parents are asked, "Will you nurture these children in Christ's holy church, that by your teaching and example they may be guided to accept God's grace for themselves, to profess their faith openly, and to lead a Christian life?" (*The United Methodist Hymnal,* page 34).

85

That is not an easy task to assume, and most parents feel incredibly inadequate about teaching the faith to their children and youth. By involving them in youth ministry, you give them an avenue where they can live out that promise, under your guidance and supervision.

Plus, we need parents who are helping teach and model the faith. You have direct contact with youth for only a few hours a week, perhaps in Sunday school and youth group. Parents, even in today's busy world, spend many more hours than you do with their youth. If they are aware of what is going on in Sunday school and youth group, they can talk more easily with their youth about those topics.

We need the support of parents simply for attendance. Younger youth who do not drive depend on their parents for transportation. And so do you, in order to have youth present in Sunday school and youth group.

One of our major problems is getting parents involved. We have to ask for help from the faithful few who support us all the time. What can we do to stimulate increased involvement from parents?

First, make a list of the kinds of support you need from parents. Include the obvious things, such as transportation and snacks. Then identify where the weak spots are. Do you need more parents for snack suppers? for transportation to events? for teachers and leaders? Under each of the kinds of support, list the names of parents who now help you in that category. This list tells you where you need to focus efforts immediately. So, what are some strategies for getting parents involved?

1. Have a regular parent meeting (see Question 76). Here you engage parents as helpers in youth ministry by their presence. Invite parents to meet regularly, to stay informed about what is going on in youth ministry, to have input in planning for the future, and to give feedback about what has been happening. This gives parents a stake in youth ministry. It also gives you a chance to know parents better and identify areas where they could be involved in helpful ways.

2. Involve parents as occasional experts. In almost every youth ministry, there are topics presented at youth group or in the Sunday school that are beyond the experience of the regular leaders/teachers. Sometimes parents are knowledgeable about those topics. Here is a chance to involve those parents in a leadership role in youth ministry. Invite them to help lead the group/class for one or two sessions by sharing

86

their expertise and answering questions about the field. You can use the same strategy for such things as work camps/mission trips. For example, I have almost no skills in carpentry, but I know a lot of dads, and quite a few moms, who do. Guess whom I ask to provide leadership for the work project?

3. For ongoing things, such as providing snacks, send a letter to all parents explaining exactly what you need and when you need it. Ask them to volunteer for one night's supper, for support services for a trip, or for handling supplies for the youth group or Sunday school.

4. The ultimate step is involving parents as teachers and leaders with youth. People have a wide variety of opinions on whether or not this is a good idea, but for the most part it seems to work. At least one large church I know of involves parents as leaders (both presenters and small-group leaders) in confirmation, and then they recruit volunteers from among those parents to teach youth Sunday school for a period stretching over several years. Other churches use parents as teachers in Sunday school for a year or so at a time. Still others use parents as leaders and support personnel in fellowship groups. If you use parents as leaders, remember that they should be recruited and trained in the same way you train other leaders, especially including Safe Sanctuaries training.

How do we help youth develop an appropriate value system if their parents do not reinforce it?

72

To be honest, this question poses an almost lose-lose situation. Any value system you teach your youth that parents do not support and reinforce will fail, at least in the short run. It is, after all, the primary responsibility of the parents to teach and reinforce value systems. That is part of what it means to be a parent. And many parents will (rightly) resent your trying to teach their youth a different set of values.

On the other hand, some parents live and teach (at least by example) value systems that are counter not only to Christian principles but also to basic rules of civilized living. For example, some parents are involved in alcohol and drugs, are abusive to each other and their children, or do not care about the community. Even here, however, you are limited in how much you can teach youth about value systems. The best you can do is point out that there are alternative value systems to the one in which they live and then help them think about how they want to shape their own lives. This may not have any effect in the short run, but it will help youth develop their own values when they are on their own.

87

What are some ways we can be supportive of parents and minister to them?

73 Some youth ministry experts say that all youth ministry *is* family ministry. I am not sure I would go that far, but there is definitely an element of truth in the statement. So, how can you minister to parents?

The first step is to get to know the parents. Talk with them as they drop youth off at the church and pick them up. Talk with them in the halls at church, on the street, at the ball game, at the concert, or wherever you happen to bump into them. Make appointments to visit with parents in their homes (as much as you can, given your busy schedule). The goal in all this is simply to get to know the parents and what their situations are.

You begin to minister to parents out of your knowledge of who they are and what their lives are like. You are also part of a pastoral team in your church, whether you are a professional or a volunteer youth leader. Work with the pastor and others on the staff to minister to families; you do not have to be a lone wolf. Be sure you do not reveal confidences from parents as you talk with other staff about family situations, but do enlist staff help in ministry.

You can do some specific things. Regular meetings with parents of youth (see Questions 71 and 76) are an important ministry to parents. Include as a regular part of the agenda some information about youth development. Help parents understand how life is changing for their youth and what the changes mean for pressures in the family. For good resources on this topic, see this section in "For Further Reading" (page 124). Encourage parents to support one another in dealing with the turbulent teen years.

Be open to conversations with individual parents or couples about specific issues they are having with their teen. You probably will not be able to solve their problems, but you can give them some insight into adolescent development and how it is affecting youth in your group. Remember, do not betray confidences in these conversations.

What is an appropriate intervention in what we judge to be a threatening home situation?

74 If a threatening home situation means one in which you suspect abuse—physical, sexual, or psychological—the appropriate intervention is to talk with the pastor and report the abuse to the appropriate officials in your community. That is the short answer. Now let's flesh it out a bit.

You do not want to intervene in the situation yourself, since you are not trained to do that and do not want to make the situation worse.

Questions to ask yourself include these: What are the outward signs you notice? For example, is there physical evidence that a youth is being beaten? Is there a major change in behavior and attitude that cannot be explained and about which the youth may refuse to talk? (Obviously, if the youth pours out a story of abuse to you, the issues become much clearer.)

If you suspect a youth is being abused, tell your pastor. By this, I mean that you talk to the pastor in confidence about your suspicions and ask if he or she has noticed any indications. Ask the pastor to assist you in the reporting process. (In many states, you have a legal obligation to report suspected abuse.)

Obviously, reporting suspected abuse is a step you do not want to take lightly. If you are wrong, it could damage the family, both internally and in the community. But you also have an obligation to protect children and youth from abusive parents. Calling for expert help is an appropriate intervention.

How do we deal with difficult parents?

75 What do you mean by *difficult?* Is this the parent who is always in your face about the youth group? the one who loudly disagrees with whatever you say? the one who talks to other parents about his or her concerns about what is going on in youth ministry but never comes to talk to you? the one who is always pulling youth out of Sunday school or youth group for what seem to be contrived reasons?

The answer to the question is probably as individualistic as the parents and the difficulties they present. It may be, however, that the best way to deal with all of them is also the hardest; that is, to be honest with them about what is happening. You do not have to accuse or attack them; there is a better strategy. Instead of saying, "Why are you always disagreeing with me?" you could say, "I feel as if there is something more going on when you disagree with me. Is there something we need to talk about?" We would all like to say, "Do not talk to your friends about your concerns. Come and talk to me." But try something such as, "I feel as if I'm part of the problem when I hear you have concerns about the youth ministry. I would like to be part of the solution. Can we talk about what's bothering you?"

89

16 My first parents' meeting is coming up. What do I say to them?

I had the same concern about the first parents' meeting I hosted. My first concern was whether or not anyone would come. The second concern was what to say. I worked out an agenda for every parents' meeting, and it always seemed to work. My agenda included the following:

- Some get-acquainted/community-building time;
- Feedback from parents: "What do you hear from your youth?" "How are things going?";
- An update on what has happened since the last meeting;
- A look ahead at what will be coming in the next quarter, including how parents can help;
- Presentation (by me) on some aspect of the faith or on some aspect of youth development;
- Questions;
- Closing worship.

We had parents' meetings once a quarter, and we always began with refreshments. Parents took turns bringing the refreshments. Other youth directors who have had parents' meetings once a month have included planning for parent involvement as part of the sessions.

My experience is that parents want to know what is going on and how to relate with their youth. If you are willing to be open and honest with parents (always keeping confidences in mind), they will respond. Then your big question will not be what to say but how to get it all done in one meeting.

Getting Support From the Congregation

77

How do we help the congregation realize and act on their responsibilities for youth?

This is a long-term project that focuses on education and consciousness-raising. Enlist the help of the pastoral staff, beginning with baptism. In the services of the Baptismal Covenant, the questions asked of the congregation imply that every member of the congregation will do whatever is needed to help facilitate the spiritual growth of the infant (or child, or youth, or adult) being baptized. Ask the pastor to interpret the importance of that question in sermons, during baptisms, in the church newsletter, and in special study sessions about the meaning of baptism. This will not cause members of the congregation to tear down your door to work with youth, but it will build a solid, long-term foundation for congregational support.

78

How do we get adults in the church to realize that youth are important enough to spend time with?

In addition to the long-range strategy outlined in the previous question, here are some things you can do. Look around to see who in the congregation is already paying attention to youth: stopping to talk to them, showing interest in their activities, and supporting their choirs, teams, mission projects. Ask each one of these people to enlist one other adult to come with him or her when he or she talks with youth. Adults have some serious fears about relating to youth, such as not knowing what to talk to them about and not wanting to seem out of touch. Following a mentor to talk with youth can help them deal with some of these fears.

Enlist some of the real decision makers in the congregation to help you. These are not necessarily the people who hold the top offices, although they may be. They are the people who set the tone for the congregation, the ones everybody else checks with to see how they are going to vote in church meetings, in order to decide their own vote. Meet these people for lunch, coffee, or just to talk. Outline for them what your game plan is for youth ministry (see Question 92). They will be impressed that you have long-range goals and have a plan to reach them. Talk to them about why youth are important and some of the needs youth have. Then ask them to advocate for youth whenever possible. This may mean going out of their way to publicly talk to youth or speaking up in meetings to advocate for youth interests. Have something specific in mind you would like them to do. Not every person you talk to will agree to help, but more of them will say yes than no.

This is usually the spot where we would talk about the future of the church. I would not do that, for two reasons. First, we have used that phrase too much, so it no longer resonates with people. Second, youth are *not* the future of the church. Oh, we hope they will be part of the church in the future, but most of the youth in your church today probably will not be the future of *your* church. They will be somewhere else. However, the youth are the *present* of your church. This is the point you should push with the congregation. Youth are here; they are the present. How do you relate to them and help them become fully participating members of the congregation in the present? And, by the way, this means more than putting youth on church committees, although that can be important.

What church structures are necessary to support youth ministries?

The foundational structures are financial, physical setting, and educational. First, the financial structures. In many congregations, the youth are the only group in the church still expected to finance their own ministries. Look at the line item for youth ministry in your church budget. How large a percentage of the actual cost of youth

92

ministry is that amount? This tells you a great deal about whether or not youth ministry is a priority for your congregation. This does not mean that the congregation has to pay all the bills for the ski trip and the day at the amusement park. That is a different issue, and youth are more than willing to help raise those funds. That is also true for mission trips. (Many adult groups also raise their own funds for mission trips, so that is fair.) However, the church should provide adequate funding for resources, programs, and training for adult leaders.

A close relative of the financial structure is physical setting. What do the youth rooms look like? Do the adult classrooms have new furniture, while the youth deal with castoffs? Are youth rooms freshly painted? Where are the youth rooms? Are they separated from the rest of the church? This carries a subliminal message all by itself. What is the physical condition of the youth rooms? I recently visited a church where the youth rooms were in one large room that was broken up by accordion partitions that were broken. They either did not close completely or had gaping holes in them. Sometimes youth rooms are used to stash equipment that the church cannot find any other place for. This sends a message to youth.

Besides strong financial and setting structures, we need a strong educational structure. It is hard to do serious teaching in a room that has only two walls, which are crammed with bulletin boards and blocked by couches. Where do the teachers hang maps or timelines? What do they use for projection equipment? What is the support system for Christian education with youth?

How do we raise awareness among other church staff about the importance of youth ministry?

Having been both a youth minister and a senior pastor, let me say that you have to begin with the senior pastor. Is she or he aware of the importance of youth ministry? How does that show in her or his priorities? Ask the pastor for an hour to talk about youth ministry. Outline your game plan so that the pastor knows what you are doing. Ask her or him for help in specific areas. One area would be closer cooperation in such things as confirmation. Ask how you can help with confirmation education. Would the pastor like your help in knowing more about the youth in the class? Then talk about worship and preaching. Most senior pastors are not going to want to turn the worship service over to you so that youth can include rock music. But most senior pastors would be happy to hear suggestions about how minor adjustments to the worship service would make it more inviting for youth. And most of them would be happy to hear suggestions about how to use illustrations, examples, and youth problems in their sermons. All pastors want their sermons to be relevant to the whole congregation; therefore, if using a youth-oriented illustration will help, they will be happy to try. If this works, they will be coming back to you for more ideas.

If you are a paid youth worker, you and other staff, such as the Christian education director and the music director, may need to talk about common areas of responsibility: Sunday school, confirmation, and so forth. How does your game plan fit with the game plan for Christian education and music ministry? How can you work together to make all programs stronger and more appealing to youth? One of the biggest problems I had when I was teaching youth Sunday school was that the music director wanted the youth released early from Sunday school so that they could warm up for half an hour before they sang in the worship service. Ultimately, we had a confrontation about that issue. However, we both came away feeling that we had learned from each other and were willing to support what the other person wanted.

In short, one of the best ways to work with other church staff is to focus on areas of common interest. If you can devise a strategy for working with other staff that leads to a win-win situation, they will be more willing to support your ministry while you support theirs.

81 What can you, as a layperson, do if you think the church is making poor decisions relative to youth, but you are not on the right committee?

If you know someone who is on the right committee, lobby with him or her. If you do not know anyone on the committee, talk to the pastor and to the movers and shakers in the congregation. (See Question 78 for ways to identify those people.) Be honest about your concerns, but do not call names or cast blame. Say things such as, "I am concerned that the youth are spending all their time doing fun stuff instead of learning about God." Make suggestions for what kinds of decisions you think would be the right ones. Ask for advice on how you could be a successful advocate for youth. Volunteer to be a part of the group (or groups) that make those decisions.

94

82 How do we help youth feel significant to others in the congregation—that is, how do we help adults (besides family or close friends) know youth by name and take an interest in them?

Begin by asking the mentors of the confirmation class to keep in touch with youth after confirmation. This does not have to be a major commitment. They could stop to talk to youth in church: "How's it going?" "What's new at school?" "What are you doing that's cool for you?" They could remember birthdays. They could on occasion invite the youth for dinner, for a Coke, or for whatever. However, they should always follow your church's Safe Sanctuaries policies and procedures (see Questions 69 and 97).

Enlist older members of the congregation. They care about youth and often have time, although they may think they are too old to do anything to help youth. Invite them to make friends with youth, to drop them notes of encouragement or congratulation, to send birthday greetings, to give them a call from time to time. Ask them to let the youth know they are praying for them. Nothing makes a person feel more significant than knowing someone is praying for him or her.

Ask an adult class to adopt a youth class. Adoption means a commitment to get to know the youth in the class, to pray for them by name (prayer partners is a good method to do this). From time to time, have the classes meet together. Invite youth to the adult class, and have the adult teacher lead. Next time, the adults go to the youth room, and the youth teacher leads the class. The adult class can occasionally invite youth to their potluck dinner and program. A general invitation will not work here. Specific adults need to invite specific youth, offer to pick them up, make them feel welcome, be sure they have a plate, and so forth. This pairing of classes could be a rich growing experience for both age levels.

Sunday School Is Sooo Boring!

To youth Sunday school teachers, the most dreaded word in the English language is, indeed, *boring*. We desperately want youth to enjoy and appreciate Sunday school, since that is the key opportunity for teaching the faith. So, when we hear the dreaded word, we automatically think we are failing, go into panic mode, and flail around for anything that will overcome the boring factor.

We can learn from good football coaches, who work out a game plan for every game. If things do not go well in the first quarter, poor coaches throw their game plan out the window and try anything that will help them get back into the game. Good coaches make adjustments, but they do not abandon their game plan. In fact, some coaches script their first fifteen plays; then they run those plays, no matter what. The game plan gives good coaches, and good teams, a sense of security. The game plan is something they know will work, so they stay with it.

What can Sunday school teachers learn from these football coaches? First, have a good game plan (see Questions 92 and 93). Second, stay with your plan. Make adjustments if you need to, but do not throw it out the first time something does not work the way you had anticipated. As we work through the questions, you will see how this advice works out.

83 How do we know when youth are bored? Are they by nature bored with church, and what can we do to change this?

People often think that boredom is inherent in youth, particularly younger youth. There are several reasons why. First, youth are experts at multitasking. They can simultaneously talk on the phone, listen to the radio, and do their homework. In addition, they are high-energy people (particularly younger youth) and have trouble sitting still. They can move a lot, carry on a conversation with a friend, draw pictures all over the church bulletin, and still hear every word you say. That irritates us teachers. Just once we would like to catch them not knowing what was going on so that we could get on them for not paying attention. But we never can. We bring them into Sunday school and expect them to sit still and do only one thing. Wouldn't you be bored, too?

Second, youth have a higher stake in Christian education than we are usually willing to credit. As one youth said at the beginning of the year, "I want to know everything." They want to know what they believe and to grow in the faith. But they do not find what they think they need—or they are afraid they will not, which is much the same thing—and so they are disappointed. This disappointment expresses itself as boredom.

Third, when youth complain that they do not like Sunday school because it is too much like school, we may need to come up with a whole new universe of teaching models. After all, there are a limited number of ways to teach, and their public school teachers have probably used all of them already. An increasing number of youth ministers look at that statement differently. They sense that, in many cases, the school system has already failed youth, and youth do not want that to happen to them in the church. So, they are not complaining that Sunday school is boring because it is too much like school; they are pleading with us not to fail them one more time.

Fourth, it is important to listen to cries of "boring" and take them seriously. Try to find out what youth are really saying. But always remember your game plan. You may have to make adjustments, but do not abandon the plan until it is clear it will never work. A good football coach stays with the game plan—unless the plan calls for passing on every play, and the quarterback just went down with a broken leg.

84 How do we get youth to attend Sunday school regularly?

What do you mean by *regularly?* If you mean every Sunday, you are setting yourselves up for major failure. Ideally, every youth would be there every Sunday; however, we live in a world of reality, so that will never happen. For example, some youth come from joint-custody homes, so they spend every other week out of town with the other parent. If they come every other Sunday, that is as regular as they are likely to ever be.

So, you have to redefine *regularly.* After you do that, how do you get youth to attend Sunday school regularly? Here are some basics to make Sunday school as attractive as possible:

- Be sure you have a strong game plan (see Questions 92 and 93). Know where you are going, and let your youth know where you are going and why you are going there. If they know the game plan, they will at least be intrigued about how it is going to work out. And, if they know the game plan, they can see that part of it is stuff they are not interested in, and part of it is stuff they care about a whole lot. If you point out that other youth care a lot about stuff they are not interested in, they will begin to see that there is a tradeoff: *If I sit through boring Bible study for Lindsay, she will sit through right-and-wrong questions for me. And maybe we both need some of all of it.*

- Have the right adult leadership in place. Good youth teachers are precious commodities (see Questions 52–63). They are willing to work with youth and to buy into the game plan and commit themselves to making it work. They are aware that not all youth like the same topics or like to learn in the same way, so they are willing to move outside their own comfort zones and take on new things for the sake of the youth.

- Sunday school needs to focus on learning, but there is no reason why it cannot also be fun. You may not do the same kinds of active games you would do in a fellowship group, but many resources provide suggestions for experiential learning (see Questions 20–22 and 89). A good resource will offer not only an outline for a teaching plan but also options for each step so that teachers can choose a variety of learning styles.

- The personality and commitment of adult leaders can make a tremendous difference. In too many churches, teachers make a commitment for only one Sunday a month. How do we persuade youth to be in Sunday school every week if the adult leaders cannot be bothered? Or, if the teacher is not happy to be there and wants the youth to sit down and be quiet, the youth will not have much fun and will not want to come back the next week.

85 How can we find out what youth are interested in learning in Sunday school, other than asking them directly?

You should be careful when asking youth directly about what they are interested in learning. Many youth do not know what they are interested in, let alone what they need in order to grow in faith and discipleship. That does not mean you should not ask youth or should not involve them in planning. It does mean you do not give them total control over the content of the learning process. Nor does it mean that adults sit back in a kind of all-knowing mode and say, "I know what's good for you, and that's what we're going to do, whether you like it or not."

Remember the coach's game plan (see page 97)? The coach did not draw it up after a vote of the players. He drew it up based on the abilities of his players, the strengths and weaknesses of the opponent, and a variety of other factors, maybe even including the weather. During the game, a player may say, "I think we can do X, because the guy across the line from me is weak against that." The coach may then try X. That does not change his game plan; it adapts the plan to fit the situation. The same is true for drawing up a game plan for Sunday school.

Teachers want to deal with topics that are interesting to youth, but there are limits to that approach. At one extreme is the teacher who walks in on Sunday morning and asks, "What do you want to talk about today?" You obviously do not want that. So, how do you find out what youth are interested in?

One possibility is to build in time, either on a weekly basis or on an occasional basis, for open questions. Some leaders refer to this as Open Mike, others as Silly Question Time. This allows youth to raise questions about topics they are interested in that might be outside the range of topics you would normally include in Sunday school.

Another possibility is asking directly. The danger in that approach is that you have to deal with the responses you get. If youth say they are interested in topics that do not come near the basic game plan of your congregation, you are stuck. If you deal with them, you have messed up the game plan. If you do not deal with them, you have told the youth that their responses are not important.

100

Try this instead: Select a list of topics that do fit the game plan. Give them to the youth, and ask them to check the ones they are interested in (first choice, second choice, and so forth). In this way, you have some control over the process and are not committed to ideas that youth toss out when they have not really thought about what they would like to discuss. You have kept the choices inside your game plan, but you have still given youth choices. You do not have to do that all the time. For example, you can plan for units on basic Bible and theology, but give youth choices in other areas.

86 What are good Sunday school resources? I want something that will engage the interest of youth but will not take much preparation time.

Let's clear away the underbrush first. No resource exists that will engage the interest of youth and not take much preparation time. Resources that say they require no preparation time still require preparation time. Oh, you may be able to understand the session outline by reading it at stoplights on the way to church on Sunday, but you still have to spend time gathering materials you need to teach that easy session. That is preparation time.

Let's dare to say it even stronger: To care means to prepare. If you walk into class on Sunday morning clearly unprepared, you communicate to youth that you did not think they were important enough to spend time preparing for this hour they have given you. If you do not care about either youth or that particular session enough to prepare, why should youth care enough to be present and to participate?

With that out of the way, what are good Sunday school resources?

- Good resources have an inherent structure—their own game plan, if you like. The objectives of the units and sessions are clearly stated. These objectives will tell you whether or not the resources will fit in your own game plan.
- Good resources offer a variety of teaching/learning styles that are aimed at the ways youth learn (see Question 94). Check the options for learning. Are they all read and discuss? Or do they offer a variety of ways of learning, including music, art, drama, movement?
- Good resources provide the background in Bible and theology you need for the session. The resource may suggest some other reading you might do, but the basic information is there for you in that one package.

101

- Good resources do not want you to teach for specific answers. That might be important in chemistry or physics experiments or on a history exam, but you want something different in Sunday school. You want youth to engage with the Bible, engage with the questions of life, and work out their own solutions. The way youth grow in the faith comes from using their minds and hearts, not from parroting the right answer. You may have heard the story about the leader in the children's time at church who was describing a small, furry animal that has a long, bushy tail; eats nuts; and lives in trees. When the leader asked what he was talking about, a little boy said, "Well, I know the answer is Jesus, but it sounds like a squirrel to me." Good resources will allow youth to say, "It's a squirrel, dude." When we teach toward the end of youth drawing their own conclusions, we risk them drawing a wrong conclusion. That is an acceptable risk. We just keep reminding ourselves—and the youth—that the faith they have today will be different in the near future because they will grow and face new questions from the world around them. So, we want resources that will be open-ended and encourage youth to grow.
- Good resources not only provide information, teaching options, and helpful suggestions but also state that leaders will have to adapt the resource to the situation in a specific youth class. No resource, no matter how good, can be used without adaptation to specific times and places. I have written sessions for youth to be used the following Sunday that I had to adapt when I arrived in class because youth brought with them issues to be discussed (which is another reason teachers need to be willing to spend time in preparation).

87 What is the secret for getting youth to be quiet and pay attention without making it like school?

The key is having a session that interests and involves youth. The secret for having that kind of session is hard work and preparation.

Youth like to learn in different ways, so it is important to pay attention to that issue (see Question 94). The more variety you have in learning activities—and the more you can relate learning to life experience—the more interested youth will be.

Youth like a variety of topics (see Question 85), but they also have a deep interest in the Bible and matters of faith. They are investing time and effort into being at Sunday school. In turn, you owe them the best way of presenting the most important material in the world. What do you have to offer that they do not learn anywhere else? You offer the teachings of the Bible and the faith traditions of the church. So, a critical way to get them to pay attention is to offer them those teachings and traditions. This is hard work, and it takes time and preparation on our part. But the result is priceless.

As for being quiet, chances are youth will always carry on some side conversations and wiggle around, even with the most compelling session in the world. As long as they are not disrupting others, do not worry about it. After all, they can listen to the radio, talk on the phone, and do their homework at the same time. So, why expect them to focus on just one thing on Sunday morning?

88 Why do youth complain that Sunday school is too much like school?

Well, one reason may be because we want them to sit quietly (with both feet on the floor), to read the lesson aloud, and then to answer questions that are so obvious. Just as in public school, they feel regimented and bored. Plus, they are in the school classroom five days a week, so they want Sunday (even Sunday school) to feel like a break. This may be one reason some churches have stopped calling what they do with youth on Sunday morning "Sunday school." It still is, of course, but calling it "Senior High Sunday Morning" or some catchier title makes it feel freer from the school model and, therefore, more comfortable to youth.

I suspect there is a deeper reason for many youth. They think the school system has failed them in some important ways, and they do not want the Sunday school to fail them as well. They want to be challenged, to grow in faith, and to find a place where it is safe to be and to open up their minds and try out some new, even weird, ideas. Senior highs, in particular, like to try out ideas that they think are new—and often sound outrageous to adults. So, they throw things out into the air, just to see what they sound like. Sometimes, by the time they have finished the sentence, they think it was a dumb idea and have already forgotten it. One way to grow and learn is to test out ideas in a safe setting. Youth do not always have the opportunity to do that in school, so this openness and challenge is an important ministry you can offer your youth.

89 What resources are available for youth Sunday school that will help a layperson feel prepared to answer all those questions we hope the youth will feel comfortable enough to ask?

There is good news and bad news here. Let's take the bad news first. *No* resource will prepare you to answer *all* the questions youth ask. Good resources (see Question 86) will provide enough biblical and theological background so that you do not feel completely lost. Inevitably, youth will ask questions about the Bible, about faith, and about life that you cannot answer. And that is where the good news part of the answer comes in.

The good news is you do not have to have all the answers. Oh, you would feel more comfortable if you did; but since you do not, here are some suggestions. First, tell the class that you do not know. Then suggest that you look for an answer together. The ideal situation would be to have in your classroom some basic Bible resources: a Bible handbook, a Bible dictionary, perhaps a commentary, and an atlas. With those resources on hand, you can find many of the answers right on the spot. If you do not have those resources in your room, there are two strategies you can follow. The best one is to set a time with the youth who asked the question (and others who are interested) to meet you in the church library, the pastor's study, or the public library so that you can look for the answer together (remembering all the parameters about Safe Sanctuaries; see Question 97). Given the constraints of time, this might not always work. So, the second-best strategy (and sometimes the best one) is to say you do not know and tell the questioner that you will look it up and try to have an answer the next week. (It is, of course, crucial that you follow through on this promise.)

On balance, the good news is better than the bad news. All you have to do is be willing to admit you do not know and offer to work on finding the answer. This is a winner for two reasons: one, it sets you free from being the know-it-all; and two, it sets you up as a person who is comfortable admitting you do not know, which makes you more approachable.

90 How do we encourage youth to learn to make their own moral decisions and not just mouth the standards of others?

Maybe more important than not just mouthing the standards of others is being able to make a decision and stay with it.

104

There are many good resources to help youth learn how to make decisions. Not all resources will include all the components listed in the paragraphs below, but a good one will include at least some of them.

- Is the resource more than skin deep? In other words, does the resource take youth seriously as near-adults who are capable of making decisions but need skills and information to help make their decisions informed ones? One of the great slogans of the war on drugs was "Just say no." It was one of the least helpful resources for moral decision making because it never addressed why we should say no, what the consequences of saying yes were, and what medical, biblical, and theological principles we need to know in order to make *no* a true moral decision. For United Methodists, a key resource is the Social Principles, which are in *The Book of Discipline of The United Methodist Church*. Other faith traditions have similar resources for moral and theological guidance.

- Does the resource help youth think about the consequences of their actions? One of the most helpful activities is to give youth a case study of a situation that calls for a decision. Ask them to list the options and the consequences for each option. Then push the exercise a step further by asking them to consider the consequences of acting on the consequences. The key is not for youth to come up with what you might consider good moral decisions but to learn to think about consequences—and the consequences of consequences.

- Does the resource provide biblical and theological background material for helping make decisions? This does not mean a simplistic "the Bible says" kind of answer, often with a verse taken out of context. Does the resource provide insights into biblical and theological principles that underlie moral decision making? Many of the vital moral issues facing our society are not even mentioned in the Bible. That is why youth need to know biblical and theological principles, rather than single texts. For example, when hormones are raging in the back seat of a car, youth need more understanding about the consequences of moral decision making than a simple reciting of "thou shalt not commit adultery" (no matter how true and important that commandment is). Another example is cloning. Youth—and the rest of our society—need to know biblical and theological principles that might apply to making a decision about the highly emotional, highly complicated issue of cloning. However well cloning might work in science fiction novels, youth need to know more about the issues than they get from the pages of their favorite authors.

91 Is there any topic that should be avoided with tenth through twelfth graders in Sunday school?

The short answer is, "Not that I can think of." The longer answer has more ifs and cautions than the short one, but it arrives at pretty much the same place.

If you have a comprehensive plan for Sunday school (see Question 92), you have a context in which you can deal with any topic that comes along. If the parents of your youth know what that context is—and it is important that they do (see Questions 70–76)—then they also know that questions may arise that are controversial. You can assure parents that those questions will be dealt with responsibly and in a context of faith development. Sometimes questions may arise that, for good reasons, are not dealt with at that time, but you can always make a commitment to deal with them at a specific time in the future.

Are there topics you should not plan to introduce yourself? If you are teaching in the context of a comprehensive plan, no. You have laid the groundwork for the topic, you are doing it in context, and you have planned a responsible approach to the topic, using biblical and theological resources. For United Methodists, a good safeguard for dealing with controversial topics is to use the Social Principles, setting the discussion in the context of "This is what our church teaches on this topic. We may agree or disagree with what the church says, but we always need to consider it." This is also protection for you, as a teacher, against parents and other church members who do not want you to deal with a topic or who do not like what you say about it.

Questions You Didn't Ask

92 How do I develop some kind of comprehensive plan for youth Sunday school?

Some fairly decent plans are floating around in cyberspace. If you log onto www.ileadyouth.com and search for the "Master Plan" logo, you will find four or five plans for senior high and for middle school/junior high, all of them using existing resources. The site also includes two comprehensive plans that use only topics without naming specific resources.

But what if those plans do not quite fit what you think you want to do with youth Sunday school, and you decide to work out your own plan? What do you do?

106

1. Name a team of people to help you develop a plan. The team should include teachers, parents, and youth. A team of more than eight to ten gets unwieldy, so recruit accordingly.
2. Identify your vision for what you want to do in youth Sunday school. When I began working on a comprehensive plan, I began with the question, If Jenny enters my class as a freshman this year, how will she be different when she graduates? The answer to the question was, She will be a more faithful and informed disciple of Jesus Christ. You may have a slightly different answer, but let's work with that one for purposes of illustration.
3. Be sure that your vision is in line with your church's vision/mission statement.
4. Identify what learnings, experiences, and values Jenny needs over the next four years to help her grow into a more faithful disciple. These could include biblical and theological knowledge, decision-making skills, stewardship, knowledge of the Wesleyan heritage, mission and ministry experiences. At this stage, keep the list to broad topics.
5. Identify, under each of the topics from your previous list, what specific learnings, skills, values, and experiences need to be included. For example, under theological knowledge, you might include such things as grace; your denomination's teachings on specific issues, such as baptism, Communion, salvation; being able to recite and explain the Apostles' Creed and the Nicene Creed.
6. When you have a long list of specific topics, begin to break them up into schedules for specific years. For example, under theology, you might want to begin with learning the Apostles' Creed in early adolescence and then move onto more abstract topics in later years.
7. Identify resources for each topic, or determine how you will develop resources for topics that are not dealt with in print.
8. Train your teachers how the new system works and how their part fits into the whole.

93

If we have a comprehensive plan, what do we do about important topical issues?

Some topics, because they are timeless, will already be included in your plan. Others will explode on the scene, such as the destruction of the World Trade Center on September 11, 2001. Make sure everyone understands that the comprehensive plan will be dropped like a hot potato to deal with an important current topic. However, you need to have some consensus about what topics are that important. Some topics that seem hot at the moment are not important to the youth, or the topic is no longer important by the time Sunday rolls around.

Use your comprehensive plan as a yardstick for decision making. Is the current hot topic really important enough to drop your plan for? Will it matter a few weeks down the road? In other words, do not be too quick to drop your plan for every current topic that comes along.

94 What about differences in the ways youth learn? Is that important for Sunday school?

Yes, it is incredibly important. Space will not allow us to go into details here, but much research has been done on the ways people learn. For example, some youth learn through reading a Bible passage and then discussing it, while other youth learn the same information better by creating an artistic interpretation of the passage or by listening to music that uses the images of the passage.

The key is to recognize that youth learn in different ways so that you can present a variety of activities aimed at different learning styles. Since some of these learning styles will not be compatible with the way in which you most like to teach, you will need to learn to operate out of your comfort zone when you plan a session. Good resources (see Question 86) will recognize differences in learning styles and offer a variety of learning activities. You cannot touch on all learning styles in any one activity, or even perhaps in any one session; however, over a period of weeks, you should use activities that appeal to a variety of ways of learning. You will see interest pick up as youth begin looking forward to their preferred learning style.

Old Stuff and New Stuff

95

The old paradigm for fellowship groups seems out of step. What is the next generation?

Good question. The answer is, It depends on what you mean by the old paradigm. If you mean a paradigm of food, games, some sort of lesson, and a devotional, that probably is out of step—particularly if it is one-size-fits-all.

So, what is the next step? There are several steps, actually. The next step is to develop a game plan (or master plan) for your youth ministry: Where is it you want to go? What are the results you want? How does your fellowship group fit into that plan? Once you know that, you have the outlines for the next step for fellowship groups.

Given a game plan, here are some potential next steps for developing your fellowship group.

- Keep the games, but develop them into something richer. Be sure that every game either helps build community through teamwork activities or serves as a transition into reflecting on the game in the light of Scripture and Christian faith. Walt Marcum's book *Go For It* is an excellent model for using games in this way.
- Use fellowship groups as an entry point for youth new to the church. Some churches emphasize fellowship, community building, and an introduction to the Bible and the faith. The fellowship group then

becomes a conduit for feeding people who are interested into Sunday school classes, Bible studies, mission trips, and other activities that help them learn and grow in the faith. The strength of this model is that it really does serve comers, those who are there for fun and/or who are new to the church. It can be a powerful model for attracting youth and moving them into a deeper maturity of faith. This model also has some potential weaknesses. One is that the adult leaders have to be continually intentional about inviting youth to another setting where they can learn more about the faith and grow in it. If they do not, then the whole model ends with fun on Sunday night. A second potential weakness is the assumption that youth have time to move into Sunday school, Bible study, and so forth. Youth are incredibly busy, and not all of them will be willing to take the time to add something besides the fellowship group to their schedule. A third potential weakness is related to the second: How does the fellowship group feed youth already in the church who are hungry to go deeper into the faith but who also want to be part of the fellowship group?

- Another possibility for a next step is a kind of buffet approach. You offer a variety of choices in your fellowship time. Some are common events that are aimed at building community and attracting youth to want to know more about the faith. The youth have choices for how they spend part of the evening: a four-week Bible study, a service project, or a time just for fun. Every four weeks, you lay out a new spread on your buffet and invite youth to choose what they will participate in during the next round. This approach provides for the needs of youth who want not only to be in the fellowship group but also to go deeper than the activities aimed at newcomers. It also invites newcomers to make choices about how they spend their time and if they want to learn more. The potential weakness is in the youth themselves. Will they actually spend the four weeks in the activity they selected? It *is* worth the risk.

How important is it that we know what the Millennial Generation is?

96

On a scale of one to ten, it is about an eight or a nine. Why? Because the Millennial Generation is completely different from Generation X, which means you will need to minister to them in different ways. The Millennial Generation includes those who were born between 1982 and 1999. Let's take a look at some of the characteristics of the Millennials.

110

- They are the largest generation in American history, with more people than even the Baby Boomers.
- They will be more racially and culturally diverse than previous generations. Fourteen million Millennials are children of immigrants.
- They have grown up with computers, video games, cell phones, and VCRs, so the world moves fast for them. They are used to sound bites and quick solutions to complicated problems.
- They spend time surfing the Web, so the world is larger (and, at the same time, smaller) for them. They do research for their school work at Harvard, the Library of Congress, and dozens of other sites on the Web.
- They want to make a difference in the world. They are what some researchers call a civic generation: committed to helping others and changing the world.
- They tend to be more homogenous in their natural groupings, which means that diversity and interracial and intercultural events will be harder to achieve.
- They will not automatically be more interested in spirituality. Their spirituality will tend to be a group spirituality, rather than a solitary one. This gives youth ministry—and the church in general—a key opportunity for teaching discipleship, the theology of community, the power of covenant.
- They want and need the church, but they need to be challenged by worship.
- They are interested in meaning, so they want real answers and not flip ones.
- Nearly twenty percent of Millennials in the United States live below the poverty line, and approximately 8.5 million are without health coverage. So, this generation has problems to solve.
- Ironically, Millennials also have a great deal of economic power, both in their own spending and in the way they influence family spending. This means that stewardship can become a key issue in working with Millennials.

So, what does all that mean for youth ministry? A key issue for Millennials is salvation: Is there anyone who cares enough to die for me? This will be a challenge for youth ministries that have tended to shy away from this kind of theological language. Millennials want to be where they can make a difference, such as mission trips and work camps. As youth ministries harness this energy, we also need to help youth reflect on why they are doing what they do and relate home repairs for the poor to Christian faith. A minority among Millennials want to know a lot more about the Bible and faith.

What About Safe Sanctuaries?

97 In some ways, this may be the single most important question in this book. Safe Sanctuaries policies and procedures are about protecting children and youth so that church (on-site or off-site) is a safe place for them to be. This means participating in the life of the church without fear of abuse, unwanted sexual advances, and so forth. Safe Sanctuaries is also about protecting adults who work with youth from unwarranted accusations. It is for the common good.

A Safe Sanctuaries program will include both *policy* and *procedure*. Policy is the structure in which the issues are spelled out. It answers the questions about who, what, and why. Procedures spell out how your church implements the policy. It answers the questions about when, where, and how. Your congregation should have both policies and procedures in place, in a written statement, so that everyone knows exactly what they are. In fact, if you are a United Methodist congregation, you may already be required to have a policy on file with the district superintendent. Annual conferences have statements of policy and procedure, as do camps and youth events at conference and national levels.

Safety measures include such things as doing background checks, having at least two unrelated adults in all groups, leaving doors open or having windows in doors, requiring that adults in supervisory roles be at least five years older than the youth. Regular training (on an annual basis) for youth workers is an important part of the system.

If your congregation does not have a Safe Sanctuaries policy in place, spearhead the development of one. The annual conference or district office has policies on file that you could use as a model. Also check out the book *Safe Sanctuaries for Youth* in "For Further Reading" (page 125).

Again, this may be the single most important question in the whole book. Because youth ministry is so incarnational, the way we treat youth is crucial to our ministry. And because youth ministry is so incarnational, youth leaders become more vulnerable and open to false accusations. Do everything in your power to protect both your youth and the adults who work with them. Be sure you have Safe Sanctuaries policies and procedures in place, and be sure that the proper safety measures are followed in all groups, at all times.

98 What are gifts and graces for youth ministry?

What do we mean by gifts and graces? These are God-given attributes, personality traits, skills, and talents that equip people for youth ministry. Gifts and graces are given both to professional youth ministers and to lay volunteers. As Jesus, Paul, and James all said in different ways, God is no respecter of people, so gifts are given to all. In both Romans 12 and 1 Corinthians 12, Paul says that gifts are given for the sake of the church, not for the sake of the individual. So, gifts and graces are what God gives us—and what God expects us to use in ministry to others.

Having said that, what are some gifts and graces for youth ministry? One from Paul's lists is teaching. It is important that we teach youth the faith, both its content and what it means for our daily lives. It is important that we teach them in love, allowing them to grow and develop in God's good time. It is important that we teach them with honest openness, allowing them to form their own understanding of the Bible and theology, rather than imposing on them a preconceived agenda of what faith is. A person to whom God has given the gift of teaching is blessed with both gift and calling and is a priceless treasure for youth ministry.

Other gifts and graces include openness, the ability to listen without judging, patience, love, honesty, and compassion. Most of those are self-explanatory, but let me say a word or two about love. Love means caring about youth for who they are, as they are; being willing to accept youth without conditions; and caring enough to push youth to move beyond inappropriate behavior, to push them to become better than they are. The following is an example not related to youth ministry in the church: At the end of my junior year in high school, I had to turn in a topic for my senior paper. Being infatuated with baseball, I submitted Babe Ruth as my topic. The biology teacher, who also taught junior English and was sponsor for the yearbook (I went to a small high school), came to me and suggested that I was capable of doing a paper on a topic that was more significant and required more thought and reflection than a biography of an athlete. She pretty much pushed me to change my topic. I now understand that she was pushing me to become better than I was, challenging me to grow and develop. Love also means, at times, being tough with youth. It means allowing them to face and deal with the consequences of their own actions, but standing with them and supporting them as they do that. We do not solve their problems for them or take their punishment on ourselves, but we also do not turn our backs on them when they need us the most.

99 I feel driven to work with youth. Is that a call to ministry?

I would say yes, assuming that your drive comes from wanting to minister to youth, not to meet your own needs. I once knew a youth worker who felt a strong call to work with youth, but that was because she needed to relive her own adolescence. Her call was to meet her own needs, not the needs of youth. Until she worked through that need to relive her own youth, her ministry suffered.

With that caution, yes, your feelings of being driven are probably a genuine call. As many people have said, a call comes when our abilities to help intersect with the needs of the world. Do you have gifts and graces for youth ministry (see Question 98)? Do your gifts and graces fit with the needs of youth in your community and church? If you answer yes to those questions, then you are probably experiencing a genuine call.

Remember, not every call to ministry is a call to full-time, professional ministry. It may be a call to minister to youth through teaching a Sunday school class, working with a fellowship group, teaching and supervising carpentry skills in a work camp. Calls to ministry with youth are not limited by age. One of the most effective youth ministers I ever knew was an eighty-two-year-old woman who, in a medium-size church, made it her business to know all of the youth by name, to talk to them and ask them about what was going on in their lives, to send them birthday cards, and to encourage them whenever they participated in worship leadership. She was not on the official roster of youth ministers in that congregation, but she was an incredibly effective youth minister. Another great youth minister taught English in the high school. Her ministry was loving students, helping them grow in knowledge and responsibility and, incidentally, in faith. She showed the love of Christ by her every action and concern for youth. When asked about important influences on their life and faith, many youth at church named that teacher.

For Professionals Only

How do I know when it is time to leave?

100 In a group of long-term youth ministers, the answer to the question was, "Don't worry; you'll know." That is probably true but not helpful. What are some indications that it is time to leave?

First, asking when it is time to leave may be the wrong question. When we begin a ministry in a church, it should be with the expectation that we will be in that church the rest of our lives. We probably will not be, but that attitude will help us settle in for the long haul. This is important because the time to leave is usually not nearly as soon as we may think it is.

Second, you will begin to get external clues. The senior pastor is often a good barometer. Is he or she more critical of your work? Are issues cropping up that cannot be talked out easily? The staff-parish committee also gives you clues when they do your annual evaluation. You should have one member of the staff-parish committee assigned as your ear on the committee. He or she should be a person to whom you can talk freely and honestly about what is happening. If this person begins to raise issues about your work or reflects back to you concerns that you are beginning to have, this may be an indication that you are approaching the time to leave. Support from youth, parents, and the congregation is also a barometer for how things are going. All of these, taken together, give you some clues that it may be time to consider a change.

Third, you have some internal clues. Pastors often say, "Have I done all I can do in this congregation, without having to push so hard that my work will be destructive?" That question may also be helpful for you, but you are also in a slightly different situation from the senior pastor. In your case, you have a complete, one hundred percent turnover in your congregation every six years or so. So, your situation is continually evolving and revolving. It is easier to know if you have done everything you can if you have had long-range goals for your ministry (see Questions 30 and 92). Are there still new challenges in this congregation that engage your passions and gifts?

Sometimes your ministry in a church is going great, but another opportunity arises. You then need to engage in prayerful discernment to discover if God is calling you to new challenges and opportunities for discipleship.

How do I leave with the least amount of damage?

Let's assume that your leaving is a voluntary thing on your part and you are not being forced out. To leave with the least amount of damage, you need to be honest and tell the youth and their parents that leaving was your choice. Do not cop out and deal with their grief by blaming the pastor or some committee, as that is always incredibly damaging. Work with volunteers, other staff, youth, and parents to plan how to welcome your successor. Tell the youth that you still care about them and will always be interested in them, but you will not be able to come back for activities.

Leave a complete set of records for your successor. This should include mailing lists of youth (including e-mail addresses), names and phone numbers of lay volunteers, a copy of your long-range game plan, a calendar showing what is planned for the coming year (including specific topics and resources). Your successor will appreciate not having to come in and immediately plan for a whole year without knowing any history or the people who are involved. The new person may want to make changes to fit her or his style, but she or he will have a beginning point and will not have to reinvent the wheel the first three weeks on the job.

If your leaving is involuntary, you probably have some feelings of grief and anger about the situation. The youth may sense your feelings, but do not work through those feelings with them or use them as a sounding board. If you need to talk about your feelings—and you will—talk to a

116

member of the staff-parish committee or to some other adult in the congregation whom you can trust to keep what you say in confidence. Then do all the things listed above to help the youth and your successor. It will be hard, but it is also the most healing way you can help the youth and their parents through this transition.

102 How do I work in an environment in which I do not feel the senior pastor's support?

I have been both a youth minister and a senior pastor, and I am still not sure about the best way to answer that question. Some long-time youth ministers think that the best way to relate to the senior pastor is a kind of "I won't bother you if you won't bother me" relationship. That may be pragmatic, but it is not always healthy for the church. Let's try some things and see what works out for you.

How is the personal relationship between you and the senior pastor? Can you sit down together and talk honestly about the situation? If you can, remember to use "I" statements and not "you" statements. For example, do not say things like, "You don't ever give me any support in church council meetings." Instead, say something like, "I feel as if you didn't support me on issue X at the last council meeting. Is there something about that issue that's a problem for you?"

If the situation between you and the senior pastor is such that you cannot talk with her or him, can you talk with a member of the staff-parish committee? The committee may be able to work with both you and the pastor to resolve the situation, or they may choose to bring in a professional to help the two of you work out your differences and develop a healthier relationship.

The worst thing you can do is complain to the youth or members of the congregation about the senior pastor. This causes the congregation to choose sides, depending on which of you they like better.

If neither of those two approaches works, or if you do not feel comfortable with them, then this may be a clue that it is time for you to leave.

103 I have been invited by another church to consider taking their youth ministry position. How do I know if this is a good situation?

To a certain extent, you have to rely on your gut feelings about the senior pastor, the rest of the staff, and the church as you can learn about it from the staff and from the staff-parish committee. But you have some hard questions you can ask. The answers will tell you a great deal about whether or not this might be a good situation for you.

- What is the job description?
- How does the youth minister relate to the senior pastor?
- How does the youth minister relate to the rest of the staff?
- How does the youth minister relate to the staff-parish committee?
- What is the salary?
- What is the youth budget?
- How many youth are involved in the program?
- What is the per-person budget?
- How does the congregation support youth ministry?
- How do parents support youth ministry?
- How many adult volunteers are working with the program?
- Are there funds for continuing education for both the youth minister and volunteers?
- How flexible is the schedule? Can the youth minister be away from the office (for example, at school visits) and still be considered as working? Does the youth minister have to have regular office hours (for example, being in the office at eight in the morning, even though he or she has been out with youth until after eleven the night before)?
- Why did the last youth minister leave?

This could be a good situation for you if the answers to those questions seem satisfactory to you and if you have good chemistry with the senior pastor, the rest of the staff (and you definitely should insist on meeting and talking with them), and the staff-parish committee.

Youth Ministry Websites

The list below is not a complete listing of all possible websites dealing with youth ministry. It represents some of the sites that youth ministers were finding helpful in November 2002. Doubtless, many have been added since that time. These will give you a start, if you are not familiar with the Internet.

www.cpsdv.org: This website for the Center for the Prevention of Sexual and Domestic Violence has research, data, and suggestions for action on topics related to Safe Sanctuaries.

www.cpyu.org: This website for the Center for Parent/Youth Understanding is an excellent website for cultural understanding.

www.egadideas.com: This website is a source for games, activities, and ideas; however, you need to provide a specific context and setting in which to use it.

www.gbod.org/youth: This website of the General Board of Discipleship of The United Methodist Church gives information on youth ministries, upcoming national events, important articles, resources, e-mail addresses for information on specific ministries, and links to other related websites.

www.grouppublishing.com: This website of Group Publishing has articles about youth ministry, resources, programs, ideas, and links to other websites.

www.ileadyouth.com: This website of The United Methodist Publishing House (Cokesbury) provides important current articles on youth ministry and allows you to see master plans, to browse resources and order online, to ask questions about specific issues, and to connect with staff members who develop youth resources.

www.kartoo.com: This search engine has fascinating links and is a fun website worth exploring.

www.ministryandmedia.com: This is a good website for finding discussion starters on current news, movies, and other media. It does not provide complete programs but gives summaries of events and movies and provides questions for starting discussions.

www.search-institute.org: Search Institute has done a great deal of research into education with youth, high-risk behavior, and developmental assets for youth ministry. This website has information about the forty critical factors for young people's growth and development, the latest research, surveys in which you can participate, publications, and information about training.

www.simpleliving.org: This website, which began as an alternative to consumerism at Christmas, provides alternative suggestions for simple living and helps explore justice issues.

www.youthandreligion.org: This website for the National Study of Youth and Religion, which is a research project at the University of North Carolina, provides news, research results, publications, resources, and links to ten major youth-related websites.

www.youthspecialties.com: This website for Youth Specialties has articles and news about youth ministry, resources, links to other websites, and national events and training sessions.

In addition, **umyouth@umcgroupemail.org** is an important e-mail address. This will connect you with a chat room of United Methodist youth workers, where you can ask questions, check assumptions, ask for help, share information about resources, mission trips, and a host of other topics. In fact, you help decide what the topics will be.

120

For Further Reading

Resources published by Discipleship Resources may be ordered online at www.discipleshipresources.org; by phone at 800-685-4370; by fax at 770-442-9742; or by mail from Discipleship Resources Distribution Center, PO Box 1616, Alpharetta, GA 30009-1616.

Building Christian Community
"Focusing Youth Ministry Through Community," by Kara Eckmann Powell, in *Starting Right: Thinking Theologically About Youth Ministry*, edited by Kenda Creasy Dean, Chap Clark, and Dave Rahn (Zondervan, 2001).

Go For It!: 25 Faith-Building Adventures for Groups, by Walt Marcum (Abingdon Press, 1998).

"Seeing Clearly: Community Context," by Steve Gerali, in *Starting Right: Thinking Theologically About Youth Ministry*, edited by Kenda Creasy Dean, Chap Clark, and Dave Rahn (Zondervan, 2001).

Dealing With Discipline
Setting Boundaries With Youth: How to Discipline With Understanding ("SkillAbilities for Youth Ministry" series), by Kathleen Sorensen (Abingdon Press, 1998).

Topics/Resources

Purpose-Driven Youth Ministry: 9 Essential Foundations for Healthy Growth, by Doug Fields (Zondervan, 1998).

"Theological Rocks—First Things First," by Kenda Creasy Dean, in *Starting Right: Thinking Theologically About Youth Ministry,* edited by Kenda Creasy Dean, Chap Clark, and Dave Rahn (Zondervan, 2001).

"Thinking Creatively: Beyond a Warehouse Mentality of Resources," by Ed Trimmer, in *Starting Right: Thinking Theologically About Youth Ministry,* edited by Kenda Creasy Dean, Chap Clark, and Dave Rahn (Zondervan, 2001).

"Your Master Plan: What Youth Need to Know," by John O. Gooch (www.ileadyouth.com/masterplans).

Long-Range Planning and Youth Ownership

"Focusing Youth Ministry Through Student Leadership," by Dave Rahn, in *Starting Right: Thinking Theologically About Youth Ministry,* edited by Kenda Creasy Dean, Chap Clark, and Dave Rahn (Zondervan, 2001).

Sacred Bridges: Making Lasting Connections Between Older Youth and the Church, by Mike Ratliff (Abingdon Press, 2002).

Youth in Charge: How to Develop Youth Leadership ("SkillAbilities for Youth Ministry" series), by Tami Bradshaw and Jeff Huber (Abingdon Press, 1997).

Getting Youth More Involved

Big Differences: How to Deal With Youth of Various Ages ("SkillAbilities for Youth Ministry" series), by Sharon Adair (Abingdon Press, 1997).

Claiming the Name: A Theological and Practical Overview of Confirmation, by John O. Gooch (Abingdon Press, 2000).

"Focusing Youth Ministry Through Evangelism," by Terry McGonigal, in *Starting Right: Thinking Theologically About Youth Ministry,* edited by Kenda Creasy Dean, Chap Clark, and Dave Rahn (Zondervan, 2001).

Open Doors, Open Arms: How to Reach New Youth ("SkillAbilities for Youth Ministry" series) (Abingdon Press, 1997).

"The Changing Face of Adolescence: A Theological View of Human Development," by Chap Clark, in *Starting Right: Thinking Theologically*

About Youth Ministry, edited by Kenda Creasy Dean, Chap Clark, and Dave Rahn (Zondervan, 2001).

Will Our Children Have Faith? by John Westerhoff (Seabury Press, 1984). This book is out of print, but it is still available in many libraries. Also check such sources as bookfinder.com.

Balancing Spiritual Growth, Learning, and Fun
Deepening Youth Spirituality: The Youth Worker's Guide, by Walt Marcum (Abingdon Press, 2001).

"Focusing Youth Ministry Through Christian Practices," by Mark Yaconelli, in *Starting Right: Thinking Theologically About Youth Ministry,* edited by Kenda Creasy Dean, Chap Clark, and Dave Rahn (Zondervan, 2001).

Helping Youth Pray: How to Connect Youth With God ("SkillAbilities for Youth Ministry" series), by Greg McKinnon (Abingdon Press, 1997).

Our Spiritual Brain: Integrating Brain Research and Faith Development, by Barbara Bruce (Abingdon Press, 2002).

Soul Tending: Life-Forming Practices for Older Youth and Young Adults (Abingdon Press, 2002).

The Bottom Line: How to Help Youth Become Disciples ("SkillAbilities for Youth Ministry" series), by Greg McKinnon (Abingdon Press, 1997).

The Godbearing Life: The Art of Soul Tending for Youth Ministry, by Kenda Creasy Dean and Ron Foster (Upper Room Books, 1998).

United Methodist Youth Handbook, by Micheal Selleck (Discipleship Resources, 1999).

Recruiting and Training Volunteers
How to Train Volunteer Teachers: 20 Workshops for the Sunday School, by Delia Touchton Halverson (Abingdon Press, 1991).

Purpose-Driven Youth Ministry: 9 Essential Foundations for Healthy Growth, by Doug Fields (Zondervan, 1998).

Safe Sanctuaries: Reducing the Risk of Child Abuse in the Church, by Joy Thornburg Melton (Discipleship Resources, 1998).

Safe Sanctuaries for Youth: Reducing the Risk of Abuse in Youth Ministries, by Joy Thornburg Melton (Discipleship Resources, 2003).

Teaching Teachers to Teach: A Basic Manual for Church Teachers, by Donald L. Griggs (Abingdon Press, 1980).

What Every Teacher Needs to Know About... (*the Bible, Christian Heritage, Classroom Environment, Curriculum, Faith Language, Living the Faith, People, Teaching, Theology, The United Methodist Church*) (Discipleship Resources, 2002).

Involving Parents in Youth Ministry
"Focusing Youth Ministry Through the Family," by Mark DeVries, in *Starting Right: Thinking Theologically About Youth Ministry,* edited by Kenda Creasy Dean, Chap Clark, and Dave Rahn (Zondervan, 2001).

Overlooked Allies: How to Involve Parents of Youth ("SkillAbilities for Youth Ministry" series), by Greg McKinnon (Abingdon Press, 1998).

Purpose-Driven Youth Ministry: 9 Essential Foundations for Healthy Growth, by Doug Fields (Zondervan, 1998).

"Theological Rocks—First Things First," by Kenda Creasy Dean, in *Starting Right: Thinking Theologically About Youth Ministry,* edited by Kenda Creasy Dean, Chap Clark, and Dave Rahn (Zondervan, 2001).

Getting Support From the Congregation
Claiming the Name: A Theological and Practical Overview of Confirmation, by John O. Gooch (Abingdon Press, 2000).

It Takes a Congregation: How to Gain Support for Youth ("SkillAbilities for Youth Ministry" series), by Nancy Moravec and Crystal A. Zinkiewicz (Abingdon Press, 1997).

Sunday School is Sooo Boring!
Sacred Bridges: Making Lasting Connections Between Older Youth and the Church, by Mike Ratliff (Abingdon Press, 2002).

Sunday School CPR: How to Breathe New Life Into Sunday Morning ("SkillAbilities for Youth Ministry" series), by Fred Edie (Abingdon Press, 1997).

"Thinking Creatively: Beyond Schooling Perspectives in Curriculum," by Duffy Robbins, in *Starting Right: Thinking Theologically About Youth Ministry,* edited by Kenda Creasy Dean, Chap Clark, and Dave Rahn (Zondervan, 2001).

Old Stuff and New Stuff

Go For It!: 25 Faith-Building Adventures for Groups, by Walt Marcum (Abingdon Press, 1998).

Making God Real for a New Generation: Ministry With Millennials Born From 1982 to 1999, by Craig Kennet Miller and MaryJane Pierce Norton (Discipleship Resources, 2003).

Millennials Rising: The Next Great Generation, by Neil Howe and William Strauss (Vintage Books, 2000).

NextChurch.Now: Creating New Faith Communities, by Craig Kennet Miller (Discipleship Resources, 2000).

Safe Sanctuaries: Reducing the Risk of Child Abuse in the Church, by Joy Thornburg Melton (Discipleship Resources, 1998).

Safe Sanctuaries for Youth: Reducing the Risk of Abuse in Youth Ministries, by Joy Thornburg Melton (Discipleship Resources, 2003).